# Implementation

*This volume is sponsored by the*
**OAKLAND PROJECT**
*University of California, Berkeley*

# Implementation

HOW GREAT EXPECTATIONS IN WASHINGTON
ARE DASHED IN OAKLAND;

OR,

WHY IT'S AMAZING THAT FEDERAL PROGRAMS WORK AT ALL
THIS BEING A SAGA OF THE
ECONOMIC DEVELOPMENT ADMINISTRATION

AS TOLD BY

TWO SYMPATHETIC OBSERVERS WHO SEEK TO BUILD MORALS
ON A FOUNDATION OF
RUINED HOPES

## Jeffrey L. Pressman

AND

## Aaron Wildavsky

UNIVERSITY OF CALIFORNIA PRESS
BERKELEY, LOS ANGELES, LONDON

University of California Press
Berkeley and Los Angeles, California

University of California Press, Ltd.
London, England

First Paperback Edition, 1974

ISBN: 0-520-02269-6 ( cloth-bound )
0-520-02759-0 ( paper-bound )
Library of Congress Catalog Card Number: 72-78949

Printed in the United States of America

4 5 6 7 8 9 0

For Kate,
a partner in program negotiation,
and for Judy,
who accomplishes, fulfills, produces, performs,
executes, achieves, completes,
and otherwise implements

¹im•ple•ment [fr. *implementum* action of filling up, fr. *implēre* to fill up, finish (fr. *in-* + *plēre* to fill) + *-mentum* -ment—more at FULL]

²im•ple•ment 1a: to carry out: ACCOMPLISH, FULFILL (wondering how he might best ∼ his purpose) (continued to clamor for action to ∼ the promise—*N.Y. Times*) (a committee to ∼ the plans so well formulated); *esp*: to give practical effect to and ensure of actual fulfillment by concrete measures (failure to carry out and ∼ the will of the majority —Clement Attlee) (an agency created to ∼ the recommendation of the committee) (programs to ∼ our foreign policy)

[From *Webster's Third New International Dictionary of the English Language,* unabridged, Philip B. Gove, ed. in chief (Springfield, Massachusetts: G. & C. Merriam Co., 1969), pp. 1134–1135.]

To IMPLEMENT: *Produce*: do; carry out; perform; execute; achieve; accomplish. *Complete*: effectuate; realize; bring about.

[Selected synonyms from *Roget's Thesaurus of English Words and Phrases,* revised edition (New York: St. Martin's Press, 1964.)]

# The Oakland Project

At a time when much is said but little is done about the university's relationship to urban problems, it may be useful for those who are looking for ways of relating the university to the city to take a brief look at the Oakland Project of the University of California, which combined policy analysis, service to city officials and community groups, action in implementing proposals, training of graduate students, teaching new undergraduate courses, and scholarly studies of urban politics. The"university" is an abstraction, and as such it exists only for direct educational functions, not for the purpose of doing work within cities. Yet there are faculty members and students who are willing to devote large portions of their time and energy to investigating urban problems and to making small contributions toward resolving them. Our cities, however, do not need an invasion of unskilled students and professors. There is no point in hurtling into the urban crisis unless one has some special talent to contribute. After all, there are many people in city government—and even more on street corners—who are less inept than untrained academics. University people must offer the cities the talent and resources which they need and which they could not get otherwise.

In 1965 a group of graduate students and faculty members at the University of California at Berkeley became involved in a program of policy research and action in the neighboring city of Oakland. As members of the Oakland Project, they tried to meet some of the city's most pressing analytical needs and also to make suggestions that could be implemented.

Members of the project made substantial time commitments (usually about two years) to working in a particular Oakland city agency. Normal working time was two days a week, although special crisis situations in the city sometimes necessitated much larger blocks of time. Since project members worked with city officials and remained in the city to help implement the suggestions they made, they avoided the "hit-and-run" stigma that members of city agencies often attach to outsiders. By attempting first to deal with problems as city officials understand them, project members developed the necessary confidence to be asked to undertake studies with broader implications.

The Oakland Project became a point of communication for individuals and groups in the city of Oakland and throughout the University of California. Its focus expanded from a concentration on city budgeting to a wide range of substantive policies and questions of political process; for example, revenue, police, personnel, federal aid, education, libraries, and the institutionalization of policy analysis. The Project provided assistance to governmental (mayor, city manager, chief of police, head of civil service, superintendent of schools) and nongovernmental (community group) actors. In order to transmit the knowledge gained, Oakland Project members taught courses—open to both undergraduate and graduate students—dealing with urban problems and policies. The Project's scholarly objective is to improve policy analysis by providing new ways of understanding decisions and outcomes that affect cities. Its members have based numerous research essays on their experience in the city. It is hoped that the books in this series will be another means of transmitting what they have learned to a wider audience.

AARON WILDAVSKY

# Contents

# Participants

---

ECONOMIC DEVELOPMENT ADMINISTRATION

EUGENE P. FOLEY *Assistant Secretary of Commerce, head of EDA, 1965–66*

ROSS D. DAVIS *Assistant Secretary of Commerce, head of EDA, 1966–69*

ROBERT PODESTA *Assistant Secretary of Commerce, head of EDA, 1969–*

RICHARD L. SINNOTT *Deputy Assistant Secretary of Commerce and deputy to Podesta, 1969–*

AMORY BRADFORD *Foley's special representative in Oakland, 1966*

ANDREW J. BENNETT *Member, Oakland task force, 1966*

DOUGLAS H. COSTLE *Member, Oakland task force, 1966*

RICHARD DASCHBACH *Member, Oakland task force, 1966*

ANNE GOULD *Member, Oakland task force, 1966*

GEORGE T. KARRAS *Member, Oakland task force, 1966, and presently director of the EDA public works division*

CHARLES J. PATTERSON *EDA Oakland Representative, 1967–68*

HUGH TAYLOR *EDA Oakland Representative, 1968–*

CITY OF OAKLAND

JOHN C. HOULIHAN *Mayor, 1961–66*

JOHN H. READING *Mayor, 1966–*

JEROME KEITHLEY *City Manager, 1966–1972*

PORT OF OAKLAND

BEN NUTTER *Executive Director*

WORLD AIRWAYS

EDWARD DALY *President*

# Preface

Late in 1968 our attention was drawn to the Economic Development Administration's employment effort in Oakland by the appearance of a book with the arresting title, *Oakland's Not for Burning*. Written by a major participant in the EDA's Oakland venture,[1] the book appeared to suggest that the city had recently been saved from riot and ruin by the infusion of $23 million in federal funds. Because it created minority employment—thus sending out a beacon light of hope to a troubled nation—the EDA program was touted as a model worthy of imitation. Since Oakland Project members were not aware that the city had been delivered from evil, we inquired into the status of the program and discovered that in 1969, three years after it began, approximately $3 million had actually been spent. At that rate, another twenty years would pass before this emergency operation would have spent the money to create the jobs to employ the people who would prevent (or at least not participate in) riots. Part of the $3 million had gone to the city for the Hegenberger overpass to the coliseum (which we somehow thought would have been built anyway), and the rest had been spent on architects' fees. We indulged briefly in mild fantasies depicting local architects about to overthrow the Oakland City Council in a suave coup d'etat, only to be bought off at the last minute by EDA funds. But further investi-

1. Amory Bradford, *Oakland's Not for Burning* (New York: McKay, 1968).

gation suggested that there were no easy targets or evident villains. Implementation of the EDA's program was just more difficult than any of us had thought.

This book begins at the end: We will concentrate on that part of a public program following the initial setting of goals, securing of agreement, and commitment of funds. A new agency called the Economic Development Administration (EDA) is established by Congress. The EDA decides to go into cities for the purpose of providing permanent new jobs to minorities through economic development. Oakland is chosen as an experiment in showing how the provision of public works and building loans can provide incentives for employers to hire minorities. Congress appropriates the necessary funds, the approval of city officials and employers is obtained, and the program is announced to the public amidst the usual fanfare. Years later, construction has only been partially completed, business loans have died entirely, and the results in terms of minority employment are meager and disappointing. Why?

Some programs are aborted because political agreement cannot be obtained. Others languish because funds cannot be secured. Still others die because the initial agreement of local officials or private concerns is not forthcoming. All these conditions were met in the EDA employment program in Oakland, but the program could not be implemented in time to secure the desired results.

In our study of implementation, we have deliberately chosen case material in which dramatic elements that are essentially self-explanatory are ruled out. There was no great conflict. Everyone agreed. There was only minimum publicity. The issue was not one of overriding political importance. Essential funds were on hand at the right time. The evils that afflicted the EDA program in Oakland were of a prosaic and everyday character. Agreements had to be maintained after they were reached. Numerous approvals and clearances had to be obtained from a variety of participants. Failure to recognize that these perfectly ordinary circumstances present serious obstacles to implementation inhibits learning. If one is always looking for unusual circumstances and dramatic events, he cannot appreciate how difficult it is to make the ordinary happen.

People now appear to think that implementation should be easy; they are, therefore, upset when expected events do not occur or turn out badly. We would consider our effort a success if more people began with the understanding that implementation, under the best of circumstances, is exceedingly difficult. They would, therefore, be pleasantly surprised when a few good things really happened.

Implementation in recent years has been much discussed but rarely studied. Presidents and their advisers, department secretaries and their subordinates, local officials and groups in their communities complain that good ideas are dissipated in the process of execution. Yet, except for an excellent book by Martha Derthick,[2] we have not been able to locate any thoroughgoing analysis of implementation.[3] Complaints about implementation do not constitute serious efforts to grapple with the problem.

No doubt a comparative approach to problems of implementation would ideally be preferable to the one we have adopted. But not enough is known about the subject to develop appropriate categories, and there is no previous literature on which to rely for guidance. We do not make any claim to have undertaken a comprehensive analysis of implementation. We are not certain we know what all the problems are, let alone provide solutions to them. But a start must be made somewhere and we hope this is it.

Implementation, to us, means just what Webster and Roget say it does: to carry out, accomplish, fulfill, produce, complete. But what is it that is being implemented? A policy, naturally. There must be something out there prior to implementation; otherwise there would be nothing to move toward in the process of implementation. A verb like "implement" must have an object like "policy." But policies normally contain both goals and the means for achieving them. How, then, do we distinguish between a policy and its implementation?

In everyday discourse we use policy (when referring to decisions)

2. Martha Derthick, *New Towns In-Town* (Washington, D.C.: Urban Institute, 1972).

3. The splendid account of the Elementary and Secondary Education Act by Stephen Bailey and Edith Mosher reveals acute sensitivity to problems of implementation. But it is not their purpose to analyze implementation as a distinct phenomenon. See their *ESEA: The Office of Education Administers a Law* (Syracuse: Syracuse University Press, 1968). Jerome T. Murphy, in the article "Title I of ESEA: The Politics of Implementing Federal Education Reform," *Harvard Educational Review* 41 (1971): 35–63, does address himself directly to the question of implementation. Although this article does not contain as thoroughgoing an analysis of implementation as is found in the Derthick study, the author does provide a number of insights into the problem.

in several strikingly different ways. Sometimes policy means a statement of intention: Our policy is to increase employment among minorities. Policy here is treated as a broad statement of goals and objectives. Nothing is said about what might be done or whether anything has been or will be done to accomplish that purpose. Other times we speak of policy as if it were equivalent to actual behavior: Our policy is to hire minorities, meaning that we actually do hire them. Policy in this sense signifies the goal and its achievement. Both these meanings of policy rule out the possibility of studying implementation. When policy remains a disembodied objective, without specifying actors or the acts in which they must engage to achieve the desired result, there is no implementation to study. When the statement of the objective includes its attainment, implementation is unnecessary.

We can work neither with a definition of policy that excludes any implementation nor one that includes all implementation. There must be a starting point. If no action is begun, implementation cannot take place. There must also be an end point. Implementation cannot succeed or fail without a goal against which to judge it.

Let us agree to talk about policy as a hypothesis containing initial conditions and predicted consequences. If X is done at time $t_1$, then Y will result at time $t_2$. If the federal government, through the Economic Development Administration, provides \$23 million in loans and grants to enterprises in Oakland, and if these enterprises agree to hire minorities after spending the money, then facilities will be built leading to the creation of new jobs that will go to minorities. Implementation would here constitute the ability to achieve the predicted consequences after the initial conditions have been met.

Implementation does not refer to creating the initial conditions. Legislation has to be passed and funds committed before implementation takes place to secure the predicted outcome. Similarly, agreements with the local enterprises would have to be reached before attempts are made to carry them out. After all, the world is full of policy proposals that are aborted. You can't finish what you haven't started. Lack of implementation should not refer to failure to get going but to inability to follow through.

To emphasize the actual existence of initial conditions we must distinguish a program from a policy. A program consists of governmental action initiated in order to secure objectives whose attainment is problematical. A program exists when the initial conditions

—the "if" stage of the policy hypothesis—have been met. The word "program" signifies the conversion of a hypothesis into governmental action. The initial premises of the hypothesis have been authorized. The degree to which the predicted consequences (the "then" stage) take place we will call implementation. Implementation may be viewed as a process of interaction between the setting of goals and actions geared to achieving them.

Considered as a whole, a program can be conceived of as a system in which each element is dependent on the other. Unless money is supplied, no facilities can be built, no new jobs can flow from them, and no minority personnel can be hired to fill them. A breakdown at one stage must be repaired, therefore, before it is possible to move on to the next. The stages are related, however, from back to front as well as from front to back. Failure to agree on procedures for hiring minorities may lead the government to withhold funds, thus halting the construction. Program implementation thus becomes a seamless web.

Policies imply theories. Whether stated explicitly or not, policies point to a chain of causation between initial conditions and future consequences. If X, then Y. Policies become programs when, by authoritative action, the initial conditions are created. X now exists. Programs make the theories operational by forging the first link in the causal chain connecting actions to objectives. Given X, we act to obtain Y. Implementation, then, is the ability to forge subsequent links in the causal chain so as to obtain the desired results. Once the funds are committed and the local agreements reached, the task is to build facilities to create new jobs so that minorities will be hired.

We oversimplify. Our working definition of implementation will do as a sketch of the earliest stages of the program, but the passage of time wreaks havoc with efforts to maintain tidy distinctions. As circumstances change, goals alter and initial conditions are subject to slippage. In the midst of action the distinction between the initial conditions and the subsequent chain of causality begins to erode. Once a program is underway implementers become responsible both for the initial conditions and for the objectives toward which they are supposed to lead.[4]

4. After numerous discussions, we have come to understand why no one else has apparently tried to distinguish policy from implementation. One person says that he likes to think of implementation as problems that arise when goals are set at high levels of organizational decision but are not realized be-

The longer the chain of causality, the more numerous the reciprocal relationships among the links and the more complex implementation becomes. The first four chapters illustrate the movement from simplicity to complexity. The reader interested in implementation should, therefore, be conscious of the steps required to accomplish each link in the chain. Who had to act to begin implementation? Whose consent was required to continue it? How many participants were involved? How long did they take to act? Each time an act of agreement has to be registered for the program to continue, we call a decision point. Each instance in which a separate participant is required to give his consent, we call a clearance. Adding the number of necessary clearances involved in decision points throughout the history of the program will give the reader an idea of the task involved in securing implementation. We will perform this chore for him in chapter 5.

When objectives are not realized, one explanation is the assertion of faulty implementation. The activities that were supposed to be carried out were not executed or were subject to inordinate delays. Another appropriate explanation may be that aspirations were set too high. Instead of asking why the process of implementation was faulty, we ask why too much was expected of it. Studying the process of implementation, therefore, includes the setting of goals (policy,

---

cause of resistance or distortion at lower levels of organizational performance. We cannot force anyone to accept our choice of words or concepts, but we do think it makes more sense to conceive of "organization" in an extended sense so that it encompasses those whose cooperation is necessary for a program to be carried out. To us, it seems strange to talk of a program as being implemented merely because lower-level participants in the sponsoring organization attempted to carry it out though essential support from others was not forthcoming. Support for a program within an organization is but one stage of implementation as we understand it.

Another person claims that policy and implementation are not distinguishable. Policy includes intended effects—i.e., policy includes implementation. Hence, a policy is not real until the intended changes have taken place. Again, we do not gainsay others the vocabulary with which they are comfortable. But we think that this choice of words confuses rather than clarifies. If policy includes its own implementation, then by definition alone it is not possible to carry out an investigation concerning the implementation of a policy. The important thing, we suppose, is that there are differences between deriving goals or objectives, working out a theory of how to achieve them, embodying that theory in governmental action, and executing it as intended. We think that Webster is on our side but anyone else is welcome to translate his vocabulary into our concerns.

according to its earlier meaning) toward which implementation is directed. By paying attention to the structural position of those who set targets—top federal officials who wish large accomplishments from small resources in a short time—and those who must implement them—career bureaucrats and local participants characterized by high needs and low cohesion—we seek in chapter 6 to uncover the causes of setting targets that are unlikely to be met.

The possibility of a mismatch between means and ends calls into question the adequacy of the original policy design. Perhaps implementation was good but the theory on which it was based was bad. Could a different set of initial conditions have achieved the predicted results? To explore this possibility, we end the book with an analysis of the economic theory underlying the EDA program in Oakland. Perhaps, we suggest in chapter 7, it might have been better to subsidize the wage bill of private firms directly in order to increase employment instead of the more roundabout method of providing grants and loans to construct facilities to create jobs for which minorities would then be hired.

The study of implementation requires understanding that apparently simple sequences of events depend on complex chains of reciprocal interaction. Hence, each part of the chain must be built with the others in view. The separation of policy design from implementation is fatal. It is no better than mindless implementation without a sense of direction. Though we can isolate policy and implementation for separate discussion, the purpose of our analysis is to bring them into closer correspondence with one another.

This book is based on interviews and a variety of documents. The first round of interviewing was done by Louise Resnikoff, a graduate student in the Political Science Department at Berkeley, who submitted a narrative report of events before leaving to pursue her studies in Tanzania. Owen McShane, a graduate student in city planning, conducted further interviews. His report, completed just before he returned to his native New Zealand, concentrated on the legislative history and economic theory behind EDA public works programs. His work is reflected in the fourth and seventh chapters. Jeffrey Pressman conducted yet one more round of interviews, this time reaching into the Washington office of the EDA, and Aaron Wildavsky concluded by reinterviewing major participants.

We are deeply grateful for the invaluable preparatory work done by McShane and Resnikoff. Without the willingness of participants to share their time and information with us, this book would not have been possible. We wish particularly to thank Andrew Bennett, Amory Bradford, Douglas Costle, Eugene Foley, George Karras, and Hugh Taylor for giving us repeated interviews and, in some cases, extensive comments on drafts of this manuscript. Our colleagues at Berkeley—Eugene Bardach, Frank Levy, Bart McGuire, Arnold Meltsner, and Frank Trinkl—made useful suggestions, as did Judith May, who is now at the University of California at Davis. The contribution of Oakland Project members in supplying missing bits of information and bolstering our morale is equally important, though it is so constant and pervasive that no particular person can be singled out. Kate Pressman computed the probabilities and gave useful advice on the charts associated with them. We would like to thank Mary Ellen Anderson and the Oakland Project staff for their skill, helpfulness, and patience in typing numerous drafts of this manuscript. As always, Pat O'Donnell, the secretary of the dean at the Graduate School of Public Policy, kept the master copy and saw the manuscript through to publication. We hope that everyone who helped us will feel they have contributed to opening up sustained analysis on problems of implementation that for so long have bedeviled participants and puzzled observers.

No book that touches on resource allocation would be complete without an expression of gratitude for indispensable financial support. Part of the early work on this study was done under a grant from the National Aeronautics and Space Administration. From July 1969 to September 1971, the Oakland Project was supported by the Urban Institute, using funds made available by the Department of Housing and Urban Development. The work published herein has been supported in large part under that arrangement. During the last year the project has benefited from the generosity of Melvin Webber and his Institute of Urban and Regional Development.

Permission to reprint the Rube Goldberg cartoons comes from the King Features Syndicate and by courtesy of the Bancroft Library, University of California, Berkeley, where we spent many pleasurable hours.

# 1

## Appearances

On the morning of April 25, 1966, the *Wall Street Journal* ran the
following headline: "Urban Aid Kickoff: Administration Se-
lects Oakland as First City in Rebuilding Program."[1] The
*Journal* article expressed surprise at the fact that "the Great Society's
first package of aid in its drive to save the cities" would "not go to
New York, Chicago, Los Angeles or another major metropolis whose
poverty and racial tensions have erupted into public demonstration
or riot." Rather, the aid would "go to Oakland, California—a city
of high unemployment and racial unrest that Federal agents have
tabbed a potential powder keg." To help solve the problems of unemployment and racial unrest, the new program would finance public works and business loans that would lead to the creation of jobs
for the unemployed, primarily blacks.

A further surprise, according to the *Journal,* was that the "donor
will not be the new Department of Housing and Urban Development.
. . . It will be an agency with rural antecedents and primarily a
rural jurisdiction: The Economic Development Administration of
the Department of Commerce. Eugene P. Foley, the enthusiastic,
restless and imaginative Assistant Secretary of Commerce who heads
EDA, will make the formal announcement this week."

On April 29, Foley formally announced the program at a press
conference held at the Oakland airport. Governor Edmund G. Brown

1. *The Wall Street Journal,* April 25, 1966, p. 1.

*I*

of California introduced Foley as "the Assistant Secretary of Commerce for Economic Development, who has decided to conduct in Oakland a massive experiment in solving the principal urban problem, unemployment."[2] Foley then read his statement to the press. After discussing Oakland's problems—including an unemployment rate of 8.4 percent, more than twice the national average—Foley announced that the EDA had agreed to offer public works grants and loans amounting to $23,289,000 for various projects in the city. The following public works projects would receive EDA money:

| | |
|---|---:|
| Airport hangar and support facilities (Port of Oakland; to be leased by World Airways) | $10,650,000 |
| Marine Terminal and access roads (Port of Oakland) | 10,125,000 |
| 30-acre industrial park (Port of Oakland) | 2,100,000 |
| Access road to coliseum area (city of Oakland) | 414,000 |
| TOTAL | $23,289,000 |

Foley said that these projects would provide 2,200 jobs when completed, with more jobs following from later "spinoffs." In addition, $1,600,000 for business loans then being considered would create 800 new jobs. Thus, he promised some 3,000 jobs in all.

But how would the EDA make sure that the new jobs would go to the unemployed residents of the inner city who were supposed to be the beneficiaries of the new program? Foley unveiled an innovative procedure: each employer who wished to receive an EDA loan or lease an EDA-financed facility would have to draw up an employment plan. This plan would project the future employment opportunities that would result from EDA financing and would commit the employer to make a concerted effort to recruit hard-core unemployed Oakland residents to fill those positions. An employment review board, including representatives of business, labor, and the poor, would have to review each plan before the EDA could provide a loan or rule favorably on a lease agreement. (In each case, the EDA itself would have to give final approval to the plan.) Every employer would submit a monthly report on hiring to the review board. If the EDA made a finding of noncompliance and subsequent negotiation failed to resolve the dispute, then the matter would be settled by arbitration. Thus, EDA financial aid would be conditioned on performance

2. Quoted in Amory Bradford, *Oakland's Not for Burning* (New York: McKay, 1968), p. 123.

by employers. Hopes in both Washington and Oakland for a successful urban experiment were high.

In 1968, over two years after the initial EDA announcement, a book appeared which suggested that the experiment had resulted in some substantial achievements. Entitled *Oakland's Not for Burning,* the book was written by Amory Bradford, the former vice-president of the *New York Times* who had served as Foley's special representative in Oakland during the first months of the program. Through a series of moving passages, Bradford painted a picture of the hopelessness and rage he had found in the Oakland ghetto when he arrived there in December 1965. One black leader told Foley and Bradford at an early meeting that "We hate Whitey because he hates us, thinks us no better than dogs. Call me 'Nigger,' it gives me respect. I have no respect for Whites, because they have no respect for me. I just want to be considered human. I'm not responsible for five hundred years of history, but for getting justice now. If we don't get it, we'll have a Watts here, and kill and bomb."[3]

In countless meetings with ghetto residents, labor and business leaders, educators, and government officials, Bradford and his EDA staff tried to break down the barriers of distrust and suspicion that divided the groups. To each, Bradford argued that the EDA could provide vital help in the effort to create jobs for the hard-core unemployed—the key to solving the urban crisis.

Toward the end of the book, Bradford provided an optimistic evaluation of the EDA experiment. He noted that "so many of the other cities have exploded with serious riots that it is clear we face a national crisis of major proportions. But all through 1966, 1967 and the first half of 1968 Oakland has not suffered a riot. We must then ask: What happened in Oakland that saved it from burning, when most observers thought it would be one of the first to go?"[4] Bradford admitted that "there are no easy answers to that question," and he went on to say that the "EDA's purpose in Oakland was not the prevention of a riot." Rather, the EDA's mission was "to attack one of the main sources of frustration and despair in the ghetto—the inability to get jobs." Still, "the fact that there was no riot in Oakland during those years cannot be ignored, as the country inquires into the

3. *Ibid.,* p. 4.
4. *Ibid.,* p. 204.

causes of riots elsewhere, and seeks to decide on the action needed to prevent them in the future."[5]

Looking back at the social and political situation in Oakland during 1966, Bradford identified two developments that "may have made the difference" in preventing a riot in the city:

The first was the dramatic, massive EDA program, directed at the central ghetto need, training and jobs. This was an experimental pilot project, something that was not being done on this scale or in this way in any other city. It was carried out with unusual speed, and was more fully coordinated with all related Federal, state, and city efforts than is usually the case with a large Federal program. The second was the local response to this new Federal approach. Following the change in the city administration, the new Mayor, John Reading, and the new City Manager, Jerome Keithley, succeeded in mobilizing first the business community, and then Minority groups and labor, to respond with effective local action. . . .

This increasingly effective combination of Federal and local action gradually dissolved the deadlock between the ghetto and the establishment.[6]

By the end of 1968, the fame of the Oakland experiment was spreading throughout the country. An article in the *New Yorker* of November 30 cited "the allocation of some thirty million dollars to Oakland by the Economic Development Administration." The article stated that Amory Bradford, in the course of directing the spending of this sum, had "managed to break a longtime deadlock between the Oakland ghetto and the local business and government Establishment."[7] The appearance of success seemed overwhelming.

Appearances, however, can change. On March 16, 1969, a *Los Angeles Times* feature carried the following headline: "OAKLAND MINORITY JOB PROGRAM LABELED A 'PRETTY BIG DISASTER.' " According to the article, the once-heralded EDA program in Oakland had fallen on hard times:

Today, only 20 new jobs have materialized for minorities and the program is bogged down in a bureaucratic fight over minority hiring.

Critics see it as a classic case of big promises and little action.

"It's a pretty big disaster," says Percy Moore, executive director of Oakland's antipoverty agency. "A lot of commitments were made, but it never got off the drawing board."[8]

5. *Ibid.*
6. *Ibid.*, pp. 204–205.
7. "The Talk of the Town," *New Yorker*, November 30, 1968, p. 52.
8. *Los Angeles Times*, March 16, 1969, p. 8.

Although an impressive array of public works construction had been planned, only the industrial park and access road had been completed.

The *Times*'s disheartening story uncovered disillusionment on the part of both businessmen and poverty groups. Walter Abernathy, assistant executive director of the Port of Oakland, observed that "our people felt the Federal government was going a little too far in telling us how to run our business." Other critics, with a different perspective, felt that most of the EDA money would "help the Vietnam war effort rather than the poor. World Airways gains much of its revenue for transporting cargo to Vietnam and the Marine Terminal would accommodate increased military traffic."

As for Oakland's black leaders, the article found that the hopes engendered by the 1966 urban experiment were badly dimmed by 1969. Local poverty program director Percy Moore complained that "from the beginning it was business as usual . . . and conditions here are getting worse. The port doesn't particularly care about social issues in the community, and the EDA hasn't used what little muscle it has to get employers to hire from minority groups."

In the same week that the *Los Angeles Times* article appeared, the EDA office in Oakland reported to the City Council that the federal agency had invested $1,085,000 in business loans in Oakland, but that only forty-three jobs had been created. The City Council was not pleased by the news.[9]

Written accounts of the EDA experience in Oakland provide two widely differing views of the program. In the optimistic view, the program had succeeded in forging an alliance between minority groups, business, and labor for the creation of new employment opportunities. In the pessimistic view, the urban experiment had raised expectations but had delivered only meager results. As time passed, the latter view became dominant. Four years after the initiation of the program, few jobs had been created and the major public works projects—the marine terminal and the aircraft hangar—had not been built. If despair and disillusionment in the minority community were in any way related to EDA activities in Oakland, these conditions would only have been worsened by the gap between promise and performance.

9. "U.S. Invests $1,085,000 to Create 43 Oakland Jobs," *Oakland Tribune,* March 16, 1969, p. 1.

In this study, we will go beyond the appearance of quick success or abject failure that have characterized most of the previous discussion of the EDA program in Oakland. After tracing the tortuous course of the program from the time of its inception, we will examine those factors that lay behind the program's frustrations: the difficulties of translating broad agreement into specific decisions, given a wide range of participants and perspectives; the opportunities for blockage and delay that result from a multiplicity of decision points; and the economic theories on which the program was based.

Our goal is not to be Monday-morning quarterbacks, to dissect the EDA's mistakes with the clarity that only hindsight can give. Rather, we will search for the lessons—administrative, economic, and political—that can be learned from the experience of the EDA in Oakland.

The experience of this program, which began with laudable intentions, commitment, and an innovative spirit, shows that *implementation* of a large-scale federal project can be very difficult indeed. Money was duly authorized and appropriated by Congress; the federal agency approved projects and committed funds with admirable speed. But the "technical details" of implementation proved to be more difficult and more time-consuming than the federal donors, local recipients, or enthusiastic observers had ever dreamed they would be.

Promises can create hope, but unfulfilled promises can lead to disillusionment and frustration. By concentrating on the implementation of programs, as well as their initiation, we should be able to increase the probability that policy promises will be realized. Fewer promises may be made in view of a heightened awareness of the obstacles to their fulfillment, but more of them should be kept. That aspiration guides this study.

# 2

## Formulating Policy

Before we trace the tortuous path of this employment program in Oakland, let us examine the background and nature of the EDA itself. How did a primarily rural agency decide to go into Oakland— or into any city at all?

### BACKGROUND: THE EDA, THE CITIES, AND OAKLAND

The Economic Development Administration was given life by the Public Works and Economic Development Act, passed into law on August 26, 1965.[1] This legislation was the successor to the Area Redevelopment Act of 1961, which had established a program to aid the depressed areas of the United States. These were areas that had suffered the loss of a major supportive industry, either through the depletion of a natural resource (such as gold) or as the result of a shift in the structure of the economy favoring one resource at the

1. For legislative history, we are indebted to Louise Resnikoff, "EDA in Oakland: An Evaluation" (unpublished paper of the University of California Oakland Project, October 1969); Owen McShane, "Toward a Transitional Economics: A Reappraisal of Urban Development Economics based on the experience of the Economic Development Administration in Oakland, California" (unpublished paper of the University of California Oakland Project, May 1970); and Douglas G. Montgomery, "The Federal Delivery System: Impact on the Community—A Case Study of EDA and the West Oakland Health Center" (paper delivered at the American Political Science Association annual meeting, Los Angeles, 1970).

(Rube Goldberg cartoon, courtesy of the Bancroft Library.)

SIMPLE, ISN'T IT?

expense of another (such as oil for coal). The program had been administered by the Area Redevelopment Administration (ARA), the organizational predecessor of the EDA.

Other programs also had a strong influence on the Public Works and Economic Development Act. The Accelerated Public Works Act of 1962 had provided funds for the construction of job-producing public works in "depressed" areas eligible for ARA funds— as well as those other areas that had suffered over 6 percent unemployment during the previous twelve months.

In 1962 Congress had also passed the Appalachian Regional Development Act, which attempted to respond to the extraordinarily severe conditions of poverty that prevailed in the Appalachian region. Most notably, the program provided aid for the development of basic infrastructure, such as roads or flood control systems, which were necessary before any community could hope to attract industry. It also allowed for the formation of a Regional Development Commission which could plan for a region encompassing the many counties of the Appalachian area.[2]

The Public Works and Economic Development Act[3] combined features of all these preceding programs. Noting that "some of our regions, counties, and communities are suffering substantial and persistent unemployment and underemployment," the act proposed to help overcome this problem by providing "financial assistance, including grants for public works and development facilities to communities, industries, enterprises, and individuals in areas needing development."[4] The new act gave the Area Redevelopment Administration a new name—the Economic Development Administration.

Titles I-VI of the act provided for assistance to "redevelopment areas" (counties or cities of 250,000 population or over) and "development districts" (containing two or more redevelopment areas) where both unemployment and underemployment conditions had been persistently greater than those in the nation as a whole. Programs for assistance included direct and supplementary grants for the construction or improvement of development facilities; long-term low-interest loans for development facilities and for commercial and industrial establishments; and technical assistance for planning,

2. McShane, pp. 5–6.
3. Public Law 89–136, 89th Congress, 1st Session.
4. *Ibid.*, Statement of Purpose.

research, and demonstration projects. Title V provided for the establishment and funding of regional commissions.

Although the act did not rule out aid to depressed areas of large cities, it is clear from a reading of the legislative history that its provisions were directed toward the economies of rural areas and small towns. In the debate following introduction of the bill, Senator Muskie argued that certain provisions were the same as in the Appalachia bill because "since it was applicable to the undeveloped counties in Appalachia . . . it could also be applicable to other areas of the country in like circumstances."[5] Senator Yarborough observed in the same debate that "this is one bill which . . . enables the people in smaller cities and towns to share in the economy."[6]

Eligibility criteria made it difficult for cities to qualify for EDA programs. To be designated as a redevelopment area, a county or municipality would have to have registered an unemployment rate of 6 percent for the most recent calendar year. Furthermore, unemployment would have had to be at least (a) 50 percent above the national average for three of the preceding four years, or (b) 75 percent above the national average for two of the preceding four years, or (c) 100 percent above the national average for one of the last two years. In all qualifying time periods, the jobless rate must have exceeded 6 percent.[7]

Although parts of cities might have qualified on the basis of distressing unemployment statistics, eligibility had to be gained on the basis of city-wide figures. (In recent years, the criteria have been changed to make it easier for cities—or parts of cities—to qualify.[8]) Thus, in 1966 only eight cities of over 250,000 population—Oakland, San Diego, Philadelphia, Newark, Miami, Cleveland, Toledo, and Buffalo—were eligible for EDA programs.

Legislative eligibility requirements did not constitute the only constraint limiting the EDA's urban role. From the beginning, the

5. *Congressional Record,* U.S. Senate, May 26, 1965, p. 11795. Quoted in McShane, p. 81.

6. *Ibid.,* p. 11793.

7. *Public Works and Economic Development Act,* Sec. 401.

8. The "Javits-Farbstein Amendment" of 1967 designated as "redevelopment areas" those parts of cities that were eligible for OEO special impact programs. In 1969, a further amendment was passed that would allow the secretary of commerce to designate areas that exhibited characteristics of dependency, chronic unemployment, or rising community tensions. (See Montgomery, pp. 8–11.)

Federal Bureau of the Budget (now Office of Management and Budget) has taken a skeptical view of the EDA's involvement in large cities. A Budget Bureau official put the case clearly during a 1970 interview:

The EDA said to us, "There's so much to be done in the cities—we've got to get involved." But we've got a lot of programs already for cities—in HUD, HEW, and so on. The EDA just does not have the resources to become involved in cities. Their budget is a small one. [In 1966 the EDA appropriation was $332,421,000; in 1967 it was $295,816,000; in 1968, $274,834,000.] If they do get involved in urban programs, to do the job right they'd have to spend a huge hunk of money in one city. A program like the Oakland one could take up 10 percent of the agency's budget. Spending that much would be politically disastrous.

This official identified a distinctive role for the EDA:

Nobody's doing much in terms of middle-sized cities. You have Agriculture helping rural areas, you have HUD helping urban areas, but what about middle-sized cities? Say 2 to 5,000 to 150,000. This was an area that appeared to us to warrant EDA's attention. A total package of $1 million can have a fair impact on a 10 to 15,000 size city. Now, for these reasons we have tried in terms of recommendations to keep the EDA out of the cities.

The Budget Bureau's recommendations cannot be taken lightly by an agency mindful of next year's funding needs.

Seemingly undaunted by legislative and administrative obstacles, Eugene P. Foley (who became assistant secretary of commerce in charge of the EDA in October 1965) was determined to plunge the new agency into a concerted urban program. An EDA internal evaluation of the Oakland program, written in 1968, reveals that,

while many people in the Department, including Secretary Connor, viewed the EDA program as essentially rural, Foley apparently wanted to go where the action was—into the cities. Foley strongly believed that EDA should orient its program to the inner city core areas *where the majority of the nation's unemployed and underemployed lived.* (In fact, at one point, Foley believed that EDA should really be housed in HUD rather than Commerce.) His trips to Oakland reinforced his beliefs and resulted in his becoming caught up in the whole syndrome in which black people lived. He wanted to do something about it and wanted to do it in a hurry.[9]

Having decided to make a significant effort to attack urban un-

9. *EDA in Oakland, California: An Analysis* (prepared by Urban Affairs Division, Office of Policy Coordination, Economic Development Administration, October 1968). Hereafter referred to as EDA internal report.

employment, why did Foley and his aides choose to concentrate that effort on *one* city? One constraint on this decision was surely the lack of available time in which to spend the EDA's first appropriation; it appeared that the money could be allocated more quickly if it were concentrated in one city, rather than divided among a few. The authorization of $500 million had been passed by Congress in August 1965, and an appropriation of $300 million was passed in October for the fiscal year ending June 30, 1966.

During November and December, the new agency was being organized and staffed. "Very few projects had been approved" by January 1966, according to Amory Bradford, "though many applications were beginning to flow in as the new program became known."[10] Only four months remained in which to process nearly $300 million worth of projects, since any not completed and approved by the end of May could not go through the required legal and fiscal machinery in time to be funded out of the 1966 appropriation, which would expire on June 30. Bradford points out that the agency had a certain incentive to spend its allotted funds, for "if EDA failed to use all of its current appropriation, the next year's appropriation would almost certainly be cut by the Budget Bureau and Congress to a figure far below the $500 million authorized in the statute."[11]

Speaking of the first EDA appropriation, Foley remarked, "I had to spend it awfully fast."[12] An immediate major project provided a way to spend the EDA's appropriation quickly. As a Budget Bureau official observed, "Gene's decision to go to Oakland was a godsend, a smart move. This would be a big bang and it would also commit a lot of money."

Foley lists other reasons for his decision to focus the EDA's efforts on one city: "I could never have found the staff to spread around to numerous cities. Besides, I wanted one significant experiment." By concentrating a major program on one urban area, Foley hoped to achieve an early, dramatic success that would establish the EDA as a pathbreaker in the alleviation of urban misery. If the experiment worked, he would have a tangible accomplishment, visible and humanitarian, to his credit. (Normally, we would expect an

10. Bradford, p. 26.
11. *Ibid*.
12. Interview with Eugene P. Foley, July 23, 1970. Subsequent quotations from Foley are also taken from this interview.

"experiment" to include some specification of what is to be tested and how the results are to be evaluated. But the EDA's sense of urgency did not permit this kind of preparation.)

Why was Oakland chosen to be the one city? There appear to have been a number of reasons for the selection:

*(1) Previous ARA contacts and experience in Oakland.*—Because of its persistently high unemployment rate, Oakland had been designated as a redevelopment area under the ARA in 1964. In that year Oakland filed an Overall Economic Development Program, a planning document that was needed to qualify for ARA assistance. Raeburn Hay, of the ARA Business Loans Office, had gone to Oakland to discuss the kind of assistance his agency could offer the city.

In meetings with Mayor Houlihan and Norvel Smith, director of the Oakland Economic Development Council (the city's community action agency), Hay encouraged the city representatives to apply for ARA funds for a skills inventory of Oakland's unemployed.[13] The application was rejected by the ARA's Washington office, on the grounds that conducting skills inventories was a function of the Labor Department.

After turning down the city's first technical assistance application, the ARA sent Andrew Bennett of the Technical Assistance Office to Oakland to pursue other potential projects. Through his efforts, the Adult Minority Employment Project was given funding by the ARA. At that time, the project consisted of two staff members who were supposed to work with unions and businesses on job development. Although this was not a large effort, the EDA felt that it had to do something to mollify Houlihan and Smith, who were angered by the rejection of the skills inventory application.

The ARA also funded a consultant's study of the potential for economic development at the Port of Oakland, with an emphasis on marine terminal facilities. The port, which had been established under the city charter as an independent agency with authority over port facilities and the airport, was preparing applications for federal funding. At the same time, a few local businessmen had submitted applications for the ARA business loans program. Thus, when Foley arrived at the EDA, there was a "shelf" of potential projects for Oakland ready for funding. The ARA had had both experience and contacts in the city.

13. EDA internal report, p. 1.

*(2) Oakland's potential for riot.*—Foley recalls that "there was a general opinion in the government that Oakland was a tinderbox— the next Watts—the next to blow." Indeed, it was the view of a 1965 White House interdepartmental task force that Oakland was the most likely of fifteen explosive cities to "blow."[14] High unemployment, particularly in black areas, and racial tension were felt to be critical conditions that might lead to a riot.

Shortly after Foley came to the EDA, he received a number of staff papers describing a "potentially explosive" situation in Oakland and recommending an EDA program for the city. Among these was a paper by Anne Gould, the EDA training coordinator, based on a trip she had made to Oakland in late August and early September 1965. While most of the recommendations in her September memorandum concerned training program possibilities in Oakland, she also described the general social and economic conditions she found in the city.

Miss Gould's tone was ominous: "racial tension does exist. . . . there is sufficient mistrust, disaffection, and frustration building up in the Negro community to make the situation potentially explosive." But it was her view that there was still time to avert disaster "if we begin *at once* with some tangible programs that will reach the residents of the affected communities."[15] Even if the EDA's main purpose in Oakland was not the prevention of a riot, there is no question that Oakland's apparent potential for a violent explosion was an important reason for its selection as the recipient of the EDA's major urban effort.

*(3) Oakland's unemployment statistics.*—With an unemployment rate of 8.4 percent (compared to a 4.1 percent national average), Oakland's designation as an EDA eligible area seemed secure. Furthermore, Oakland appeared to be of manageable size; Washington officials felt that "Oakland's unemployed population was small enough in absolute numbers to be impacted upon by an EDA investment."[16]

*(4) Oakland's political situation.*—In reviewing his reasons for choosing Oakland, Eugene Foley pointed out that "Oakland had a Republican administration. If anything went wrong with an EDA

14. *Ibid.,* pp. 8–9.
15. *Ibid.,* p. 3. Italics in the original.
16. *Ibid.,* p. 9.

program, if we were arguing with a mayor, I did *not* want some Democratic mayor—like Daley—to be able to pick up the phone and call President Johnson. With a Republican mayor, I thought the federal government would at least not be against us." Oakland's weakness vis à vis the federal government thus became an advantage in drawing Foley's attention.

For a number of reasons—economic, administrative, and political—Oakland qualified admirably for the EDA's urban experiment. It had a high unemployment rate, and this condition—coupled with racial distrust—was felt by federal officials to mark the city as a prime target for a riot. Also, the ARA had had previous experience in the city and projects had already been developed. Finally, Oakland officials could not go over the EDA's head to the president.

Before beginning work on developing an Oakland program, Foley and his chief aides had made a number of crucial decisions—to launch a major EDA urban effort, to concentrate the program on one city, and to designate Oakland as the particular target. Let us now examine the City of Oakland and the ways in which the EDA effort there initially took shape.

## HOPEFUL BEGINNINGS (1965–66)
### OAKLAND—THE MEDIUM FOR THE EXPERIMENT

In 1966, when the University of California's Survey Research Center carried out a survey of poverty in Oakland, the total household population of the city was 365,490. The racial composition of the city, summarized in Table 1, shows a large minority population. Among people defined as below the poverty level—earning below $2,500 per year for a single individual and below $4,000 for a family

TABLE 1: Racial Composition of Oakland, California, 1966

| Ethnicity | Number | Percent |
|---|---|---|
| White (excluding Spanish surname) | 201,180 | 55 |
| White (with Spanish surname) | 35,200 | 10 |
| Negro | 110,050 | 30 |
| Other nonwhite | 19,060 | 5 |
| Total persons | 365,490 | 100 |

SOURCE: Survey Research Center, University of California, *Poverty and Poverty Programs in Oakland: Selected Results from the 701 Household Survey of Oakland,* William L. Nicholls, II, Study Director (Berkeley, 1967), p. 26.

of four—minority groups (black people and Mexican-Americans) were overrepresented. Whereas blacks made up 30 percent of the city's total population, they constituted 45 percent of the poverty population. Mexican-Americans, who made up 10 percent of the city's population, were 14 percent of the poverty population.

The most relevant statistics from the EDA's point of view were those concerning unemployment. Table 2 shows that Oakland's unemployment rate was over twice the national average. And other data from the survey showed clearly where the burden of joblessness rested. Among blacks and Mexican-Americans, the unemployment rate was found to be 12 percent, as opposed to 6 percent among whites and 8 percent among "orientals and other non-whites."[17] In the affluent Oakland hills, unemployment was 3.9 percent; in the West and East Oakland ghettoes, the figures were 14.3 percent and 14.4 percent, respectively.[18]

TABLE 2: Oakland's Unemployment Rate Is Significantly Higher than the National Average[a]

| | Percent of Civilian Labor Force Unemployed | |
| *Rates* | *Oakland* | *United States* |
| --- | --- | --- |
| *Crude Rates*[b] | | |
| Total (all civilian workers) | 8.4 | 4.1 |
| Males, 20 years and over | 4.8 | 2.3 |
| Females, 20 years and over | 8.3 | 3.9 |
| Both sexes, 14 to 19 years | 30.5 | 13.0 |
| *Seasonally Adjusted Rates*[c] | | |
| Total (all civilian workers) | 7.7 | 4.0 |
| Males, 20 years and over | 4.6 | 2.5 |
| Females, 20 years and over | 7.5 | 3.9 |
| Both sexes, 14 to 19 years | 26.7 | 12.4 |

[a]Figures based on 1966 "701" study of Oakland. Section 701 of the Federal Housing Act of 1954, as amended, provides funds for urban planning assistance.
[b]For Oakland, the sample unemployment rate based on all cases included in the 701 survey. For the United States, the mean adjusted unemployment rate for May, June, July, and August.
[c]Mean seasonally adjusted rates for May, June, July, and August. For Oakland, an approximate seasonal adjustment was made for interviews completed in each month, based on U.S. seasonal adjustment figures.
Source: Stanford Research Institute, *Human Resources Development for Oakland: Problems and Policies* (Menlo Park, 1968), p. 10.

17. Stanford Research Institute, *Human Resources Development for Oakland: Problems and Policies* (Menlo Park, 1968), p. 12.
18. *Ibid.,* p. 16.

In dealing with the problems posed by poverty, unemployment, and racial tension, Oakland's elected officials have faced a number of obstacles. One is the fragmentation of governmental authority: the Redevelopment Agency, Housing Authority, School Board, and Port Commission are all outside the control of City Hall. (In 1967 the poverty program's community action agency, the Oakland Economic Development Council, declared its independence from local government, though the city took over again in 1971.)

City government itself is based on the council-manager form, under which the City Council is supposed to formulate policy and the city manager is supposed to administer that policy. The mayor, who is elected separately, is one of nine councilmen. Although the council-manager model assumes that "policy" will direct "administration," the relationship between policy and administration in Oakland has been strongly affected by the resources available to the politicians on one hand and the administrators on the other. The advantages of the administrators are considerable.

First of all, the mayor and councilmen are not intended to serve full time at their jobs; the city manager, in contrast, is enjoined by the charter "to devote his entire time to the duties and interests of the City."[19] Salary levels underscore this difference: the mayor earns only $7,500 and each councilman earns $3,600 per year, but the city manager's annual salary is $38,940. It would be a rare councilman or mayor who could afford to spend full time on his job.

This imbalance between the political and administrative sides of Oakland city government is further increased by a disparity in the staff and informational resources available to the council and manager. For the entire city council is served by just one secretary, who answers the phone, arranges appointments, types letters, and administers the Christmas program of the Municipal Employees' Choir. The mayor is not much better off, with one administrative assistant and three secretaries.

The city manager, in sharp contrast, may utilize the manpower and information resources of all city departments under his control —police, fire, public works, and so forth. Furthermore, the manager has three full-time staff assistants in his own office who help him keep abreast of departmental communications. The finance and budget directors, who serve under the city manager, provide him with in-

19. *Charter of the City of Oakland*, Sec. 27 (4) m.

formation regarding department allocations and utilization of city funds. As a result, the city manager tends to know more than anyone else about city government structure, processes, and substantive policy. For an elected public official in Oakland who wishes to exercise leadership, the built-in obstacles are enormous.

Perhaps even more discouraging to the exercise of political leadership has been the nature of ·Oakland's political system itself. The lack of politically oriented interest groups and party activity has meant that leaders—or potential leaders—have been deprived of a source of both information about and support for public policies they might wish to propose.

EDA officials who were interviewed in 1970 felt that Oakland's governmental and political system constituted one of their most difficult problems in the implementation of their program in that city. We shall examine the connections between this federal program and the Oakland political system in a later chapter. But let us return now to the hopeful beginnings of the EDA Oakland program in the seemingly distant past of 1965–66.

FIRST IMPRESSIONS

On December 9, 1965, Eugene Foley, the assistant secretary of commerce, and Amory Bradford, who had expressed an interest in helping EDA urban projects, made their first visit to Oakland. Instead of going to City Hall or the Port of Oakland, Foley and Bradford went to a meeting of the East Oakland Parish. John Frykman, Pastor of St. John's Lutheran Church in East Oakland, had assembled a dozen people—including black community organizers and members of the parish staff—to tell Foley about Oakland. Curtis Lee Baker, an outspoken black man, took a dim view of the outsiders' visit: "What did it cost to bring you rich White men out here? We'd rather have the money. We've had enough studies. What we need now is justice, action, jobs!"[20]

Later in the day, Bradford and Foley went to a Teamsters hiring hall and talked to blacks who were looking for jobs. Then came a tour of the West Oakland ghetto, guided by Curtis Baker and Elijah Turner, a CORE officer. The overall impression they gained was a

20. Bradford, p. 5.

bleak one; blacks in the Oakland ghetto faced uncertain employment prospects and suffered from poverty and woefully inadequate housing.

A month later, on January 7, 1966, Foley and Bradford returned to Oakland. On the next morning they were to attend a "mass meeting" called by Curtis Baker to tell the federal representatives more about the needs of the unemployed. Although the recreation hall that was to have been the meeting place had been "closed for painting" (Baker and his friends suspected a City Hall move against them), Foley was able to talk informally to those assembled on the grass outside the hall.

Bradford felt that thoughts were expressed frankly and easily between the EDA officials and poor black people, and he wrote in his book:

I noted then something that surprised me, but which has since been confirmed again and again. The poor and the unemployed see their problems more clearly, and better understand the mechanisms of society that create their problems, than the great majority of outside, trained experts whose job it is to provide solutions. Also, even when illiterate, they express their knowledge with a simple clarity and force, unencumbered by complicated theory, which cuts through many useless preconceptions.[21]

Assistant Secretary Foley was also impressed by his visits to the Oakland ghetto. After the January 8 meeting Bradford wrote in a letter that "Foley is going to make Oakland a pilot project in concentrating all Federal resources to create new jobs by bringing in new business, public works, training, and ending discrimination in hiring." Foley had asked Bradford to "head this up, negotiating with business and labor and all groups involved, and coordinating the efforts of all government agencies"[22]— a large order indeed.

Why, in their initial trips to Oakland, did Foley and Bradford neglect visiting City Hall? Foley offers this explanation: "I didn't want to alienate the black community by seeming to come in as part of the Establishment. I wanted to meet black people first." This strategy, however, did alienate Oakland's Mayor John C. Houlihan, who complained bitterly about Foley's choice of initial contacts when the mayor visited the assistant secretary in Washington on January

21. *Ibid.*, p. 17.
22. *Ibid.*, p. 22.

13.[23] Although angered by the rebuff, Mayor Houlihan—who was actively trying to promote economic development in Oakland—agreed to set up a meeting of local leaders on January 28 and 29 to hear about Foley's proposed pilot program.

THE OAKLAND TASK FORCE AND ADMINISTRATIVE INNOVATION

At a breakfast meeting with Foley on January 13, the day of Mayor Houlihan's visit, Amory Bradford agreed to take over personal direction of the EDA project in Oakland. Foley assigned to the project a group of staff members—mostly young—who he felt were both capable and committed to urban programs. They included Andy Bennett of Technical Assistance and Anne Gould, the training coordinator, who had been instrumental in directing Foley's attention to Oakland in the first place. Other members of the group assigned to Oakland were:

*Jay Schwamm,* an investment banker who had been retained by Foley as a project consultant charged with increasing the role of private investment in economic development.

*Blair Butterworth,* the son of a career diplomat and a graduate of Princeton, who came from the Peace Corps in Ghana to be western area supervisor in charge of EDA offices in the western states.

*Douglas Costle,* an attorney in the EDA general counsel's office, who was Bradford's Washington liaison and then his assistant in Oakland. Costle had spent two years working with the Civil Rights Division of the Justice Department.

*Richard Daschbach,* of the Business Loans Division, who was charged with stimulating interest in the loans program. Daschbach was also a lawyer; he had begun his Washington career as an assistant to Representative Hale Boggs of Louisiana.

*George Karras,* of the Office of Public Works (and in 1972 director of that office), who was to analyze public works projects for their job-creating possibilities and technical soundness. Karras, who came out of the labor movement, was now committed to EDA service as a long-term career.

*Bill Leland,* assistant for Equal Opportunity, who was to concentrate on civil rights questions.

23. *Ibid.,* p. 29.

Foley believed that "about 90 percent of the people in government are for retrenchment. The challenge is to pick out the 10 percent who can do something. You have to move directly and circumvent the bureaucracy if you really want something." For these reasons Foley changed the normal bureaucratic procedure in order to expedite the Oakland project: "I advised my administrators that Oakland had the highest priority. Any request from Bradford had the highest priority; Bradford was able to call me directly and calls would always be put through."

The members of the Oakland task force were similarly inclined toward nonbureaucratic innovation. Bradford says,

All were the antithesis of the stereotyped bureaucrat cautiously protecting his career. Their approach right down the line was: "What needs to be done? How can we do it best, and faster?" When the answers were clear, they were all willing to risk their careers and their health and sacrifice their personal lives, to get the job done well and quickly. Something happened to us all in Oakland, once we became identified with its problems, that created a rare combination of shared dedication, excitement and satisfaction.[24]

Members of the task force interviewed in 1970 remembered the "exhilaration," "excitement," and "feeling that we could really turn things around" that pervaded the EDA project in 1966.

There were those who did not share the enthusiasm for the Oakland project shown by Foley, Bradford, and the members of the task force. Bradford admits that the high spirit of the project team "puzzled, and annoyed, some of their uninitiated associates and bosses in Washington, until they came to Oakland and caught the fever themselves."[25] (Unfortunately for the project, there were many EDA officials in Washington who never "caught the fever." The 1968 EDA internal evaluation said that "Foley's arrangement had created intra-agency antipathies between his task force agents and their program superiors."[26])

The magnitude of the departure from normal bureaucratic channels should not be exaggerated. As one task force member pointed out,

24. *Ibid.*, p. 30.
25. *Ibid.*, p. 31.
26. EDA internal report, p. 52.

Foley did by-pass people—like [Secretary of Commerce] Connor—in his decision to go into Oakland and commit the funds. But, after we went in, the paperwork, review, and analysis was done by regular EDA Washington staff. Although it is true that, in business loans, Daschbach did do a lot of running himself, and although Foley did put gold stars on certain projects he wanted expedited. My job was expeditive: cajoling, persuading, etc. I did not evaluate projects; technical project evaluation would be done by EDA staff.

It is important also to note that EDA task force members split their time between Washington and Oakland and were not relieved of their regular Washington duties. During this time they were also working on legal opinions, loan applications, and public works construction in their respective EDA divisions.

Thus, the administrative break with normal channels was far from complete, but there is no question that it engendered substantial resentment among EDA staff members in Washington. Holdover staff members from the ARA, who had prepared plans for projects all over the country, now found that Oakland had highest priority. An urban program was being initiated—and quickly—in an agency whose staff was primarily oriented toward rural areas.

DUNSMUIR

A few days before the Dunsmuir House meeting at which the EDA representatives were to confer with Oakland's civic and business leaders, one Oakland institution had the opportunity to present an early case to the EDA. Monroe Sullivan, a staff member of the Port of Oakland, had initiated engineering and architectural studies that would lead to the port's submission of applications for EDA aid. Then Sullivan worked up a brochure to present the projects to EDA staff. He called Blair Butterworth to arrange for an appointment, and Sullivan met with the EDA task force in Foley's office shortly before they left for Oakland. With Oakland's congressmen George Miller and Jeffery Cohelan in supportive attendance, Sullivan made a detailed presentation of the port's needs and its plans for meeting them with EDA assistance.[27]

When the task force met with Foley on January 26 to review the program for the upcoming meetings, a number of the staff proposed that the EDA efforts be coordinated carefully with those of all other

27. Bradford, p. 34.

federal agencies, both in Oakland and in Washington. But Foley objected, on the grounds that it would delay the project "longer than
Oakland can afford to wait." Instead, he said that the EDA should
proceed as fast as it could and let coordination follow later.[28] Foley
was fond of repeating a story about Mayor Jimmy Walker of New
York. A Democratic candidate for city council, who was worried
about his chances for election, expressed that anxiety to Walker.
So the mayor took the candidate for a ride on a tugboat and pointed
to the garbage following in the boat's wake. "You see the way this
boat is pulling in that garbage?" asked Walker. "Well, that's how
I'm going to pull you in on Election Day." In a similar manner, explained Foley, the EDA would be out front and the other agencies
would be pulled along. Prior coordination would be unnecessary.

Even if the EDA had decided to coordinate its policies with other
departments, what would "coordination" have meant for designing
policy? Who would coordinate whom? Toward what ends would the
coordination be directed? And which part of the EDA—Washington
offices, task force, regional office—would be involved in coordination?

Dunsmuir House is a stately white-columned mansion in a park
at the edge of Oakland, which has served from time to time as a city
conference center. The EDA had left the question of whom to invite
to the January 28 conference in the hands of Mayor Houlihan. He
assembled about forty business and governmental leaders, including
representatives of the port, the chamber of commerce, the Oakland
Economic Development Council (OEDC), and the Planning Commission. The newly named city manager, Jerome Keithley, was there
—as well as the heads of some city departments. But aside from the
mayor, no city councilmen were present.

Because of EDA concern about the lack of representation from
labor and minority groups, last-minute invitations were issued to
Robert Ash, executive secretary of the Alameda County Central
Labor Council, and to Judge Lionel Wilson, chairman of the OEDC.
Judge Wilson and Norvel Smith were the only blacks present.[29]

In introducing the federal officials, Mayor Houlihan showed that
he had not buried his hard feelings toward them. He said that the
city "had suffered from the oral contributions of the people in the

28. *Ibid.*
29. *Ibid.*, p. 38.

streets" and the visits of "the gratuitous activists, and the Federal Hawkshaws [who] come in and embrace the poor. All this has kept the fans of discontent going" and was "stirring in a mudhole."[30] But then Houlihan changed his tone and declared that he was "full of hope and desire" for the EDA program and ready to help it along.

Foley, somewhat angered by the introduction, nevertheless managed to keep his temper and to pledge a "creative federalism." He said that past experience with central direction from Washington had shown that it did not "allow for adapting programs to the personality of the community. Creative Federalism requires more and more decisions to be made at the local level, with only policy direction from Washington." Foley then emphasized the EDA's central mission in the city: "Our constraint, very simply, is that we must create new and permanent jobs for the unemployed and the underemployed. Here, that means the Negro."[31]

The EDA program was then presented in detail. Andy Bennett discussed technical assistance. George Karras outlined the public works program, and Dick Daschbach described business loans. Bill Leland reviewed the statutory requirements for equal opportunity hiring.

After the presentations were over, City Manager Keithley raised a perceptive and troubling question, one that would haunt the EDA in the days and years ahead: "Aren't we skirting the problem? We are getting a lot of good information, but how do you connect with the long-term unemployed? We still have not heard a formula on guaranteeing that the right people get the right job."[32] The search for that formula would prove difficult.

On the second day of the conference, Foley announced that he was "prepared to set up a pilot project in Oakland, to see if a massive injection of money can create permanent jobs for the hard-core unemployed. We are talking about $15,000,000, and possibly upward if you can spend it wisely in a short length of time."[33]

Where had the figure of $15,000,000 come from? An early EDA participant recalled that "Karras had told Foley, 'Well, you can commit fifteen million dollars safely.' Foley was wondering what figure

30. *Ibid.*, p. 39.
31. *Ibid.*, p. 40.
32. Ibid., p. 43.
33. *Ibid.*

he should announce and they decided to pick a figure they knew they could safely commit and also one that was big enough to really make people listen to them."

Oakland's civic and business leaders did listen to the EDA team, although they showed considerably more interest in business expansion than in creating jobs for the unemployed.[34] Still, given the $15,-000,000 "carrot," the federal representatives hoped that progress could be made in the latter area.

During February the EDA staff in Oakland wrestled with the question of how to tie business development to jobs for the long-term unemployed. There was no unanimity within the EDA organization on the necessity of tying financial aid to job guarantees. One field representative, who had not been at Dunsmuir, told a concerned Oakland minister that "there were no EDA regulations that required the recipient of a grant or loan to employ the long-term unemployed, and that instead it was just expected that the jobs created would eventually result in such employment." [35] Like the businessmen, he apparently expected an abstraction called "the entire community" to benefit from economic growth. Prosperity meant more jobs, and minorities somehow would share in them.

Bradford felt that a general standard of "maximum possible employment" of ghetto residents was too vague and that the EDA ought to try to gain more specific commitments. He therefore searched for a way to link the jobs more closely to the local unemployed. The task force had first thought of assembling a high-level committee that would establish and enforce employment standards. But they soon decided that such willing and able leaders were not to be found in Oakland at that time. The answer Bradford settled on was that of an employment plan in which each applicant for EDA assistance would be required to enumerate and describe jobs that he thought would result from that assistance. Furthermore, each employer would have to tell the EDA what he would do to recruit the hard-core unemployed and what training would be required. All this would be submitted to a local committee—and then the EDA—for

34. A situation that was noticed by Bradford, Foley, and the rest of the EDA task force at Dunsmuir.
35. Quoted in Bradford, pp. 72–73.

review and approval before the EDA would agree to provide assistance.

If approved, the employment plan would become part of the contractual agreement between the EDA and an employer; noncompliance with the plan would be a condition of default in the loan or the lease of EDA-improved facilities. (Several employers objected strenuously to the penalty clause which made noncompliance a default enabling the EDA to terminate a lease or call a loan. In August Bradford and his Oakland colleagues decided to substitute arbitration for the stringent penalties of default.)

The Employment Plan Review Board was an integral part of the process Bradford envisioned, for that body would both rule on applications for assistance and provide a continuing system of surveillance over approved projects.

Participation of the poor, although never mentioned in the EDA act, was important to Bradford and to some of his colleagues in the EDA. One task force member explained that "You had to have a committee representing the poor themselves. A countervailing structure to City Hall was important to recognize the legitimacy of the claims of the poor. Bradford and I had gone to a lot of poverty program target area meetings. We were impressed by what we'd seen —impressed by the eloquence of target area representatives."

Within the Oakland poverty program in 1966, representatives of the poverty target areas were fighting for and gaining a greater voice in the program. Bradford and the task force came to feel that poor people should also have the dominant voice on the Employment Plan Review Board. Accordingly, they decided that a majority of the members of that board should be designated by the target area poverty groups.[36]

Although Bradford found enthusiasm in Oakland for his employment plan proposal, some EDA officials in Washington were less happy about it. The agency's lawyers wondered about its looseness; business loan experts worried about the wisdom of saddling already hard-pressed loan recipients with additional obligations; public works administrators viewed the plan as an unnecessary complication in the difficult task of project management. Many were convinced that the whole process was too cumbersome and harsh to be

36. Bradford, p. 83.

put into effect. The final decision, however, rested with Eugene Foley. During the last week of March, Foley sided with Bradford and approved the plan.

## A CHANGE OF MAYORS

Other events were occurring in Oakland during February 1966. Mayor Houlihan was charged with embezzling over $90,000 from an estate that he, as a lawyer, had been administering; the mayor resigned on February 15. Two weeks later, the City Council elected one of its members—John H. Reading—to be mayor. Reading, a "nonpartisan" Republican, was a successful businessman who was dedicated to civic service. Though he had an intense dislike for politics, he soon gave promise of being an activist mayor.

Foley, Bradford, and their EDA assistants were impressed with Reading's first actions in office—nominating (unsuccessfully) a black man to fill his old seat on the City Council, seeking out contacts in the ghetto, and vociferously supporting the EDA and other employment-related projects. An EDA participant 'ecalled that "Reading at this time began to look like a very strong mayor. . . . We had a tremendous asset in a potentially strong mayor."

## PROJECT DECISIONS: PUBLIC WORKS

When the processing of applications begun in February, time was a pressing concern of the EDA staff. If the appropriation was not spent by June 30, the EDA would lose the money and its future appropriations might be reduced. Because of the time needed for legal and fiscal processing, project proposals would have to be completed by the end of May. Given this constraint, there was not sufficient time to carry out an extensive search of possible sponsors of public works projects.

Besides, there was one applicant that had already made contact with the EDA. "Following the results of the technical assistance project," an EDA staff member pointed out, "it appeared that the port was ready. So we immediately put together port-related projects." The port also had other advantages: autonomy, ownership of a large area, tremendous growth potential, and previous favorable evaluations by the ARA.[37] And EDA officials felt that the port was the

37. McShane, pp. 40–42, discusses these at some length.

institution in Oakland most adept in filling out federal applications. (To him that hath the ability to fill out the forms shall be given.) In any event, given the time constraint, the port appeared to be the only show in town. As an EDA man put it, "The EDA had to spend its funds by June of 1966. The port had the projects and the others didn't."

The city government did submit applications for a range of public works—sewers, streets, and so forth—but it was turned down on the grounds that such projects would not generate sufficient employment. The only city project to be approved was an access road to the newly built coliseum. This project's approval was seen by the EDA task force as an effort on the part of their agency to get city administrators to respond to the program; they never expected that the access road would create many jobs.

In Washington the staff of the Office of Public Works assessed the projects as vehicles for job creation. They made employment estimates based on known and anticipated growth of major project users. The potential recipient's job plans also played a role in these projections. Job estimates were discounted if they would take a long time to materialize or if they were unrelated to the projects under consideration.[38]

At the beginning of April, according to a task force member, "there was a ranking of all programs . . . in relation to employment. Now, for example, building the Hegenberger extension by the city, we put that way down the list because there was really not much employment in it." There was some disagreement on relative ranking; employment prospects were very difficult to predict.

Finally, projects worth $23,289,000 were selected to announce on April 29. By what process was that figure chosen? "There was a phone conversation between Washington and Oakland," Bradford says, "and we drew the line at a certain point in the ranking. There was a stop right under the ones I really wanted and above the ones that I didn't want. The cluster above the line were ones that I was really anxious to get through."[39]

38. Letter from George Karras, director of the EDA Office of Public Works, to Jeffrey Pressman, November 17, 1970.
39. Pressman interview with Amory Bradford, October 27, 1970.

In developing their Oakland program, the EDA task force had the assistance of the sociologist Floyd Hunter, whose consulting firm of Social Science Research and Development Corporation received an EDA planning advance of $72,000 in March. Hunter had been brought into the project by Foley, who says he "was impressed by his [Hunter's] book on Atlanta and by Hunter personally. I thought he could be a critical independent scholar—watching our performance and criticizing us where appropriate." Hunter appeared to have appropriate credentials, since he was an academic and recognized as a critic of Oakland's city government, having written a report on the city's housing situation that had angered City Hall. (This, it was felt, would help to keep the EDA free of the "establishment" label.)

At the beginning, Bradford thought that "Hunter was helpful . . . telling me about Oakland, being a guy I could talk to."[40] Later, Hunter would significantly expand his role in the EDA project.

THE ANNOUNCEMENT

After the successful projects had been selected, but before they had been announced, port officials expressed their concern about part of the employment plan procedure. Specifically, they had serious reservations about the requirements that the employment plan provisions be included in lease and sales of port property developed with EDA funds.

Some of the EDA's Washington staff, who had never liked the employment plan idea in the first place, argued that the federal agency should seek to reach agreement with the port on this point before the April 29 announcement. But Bradford held firm; he urged Foley to "simply announce our employment conditions and leave it to them to accept or reject the entire offer. I was certain that once the offers had been publicly announced it would not be feasible for them to reject $23,000,000 of needed development funds because of the EDA requirements that jobs go to the local unemployed."[41]

40. *Ibid*.
41. Bradford, p. 122.

Foley agreed, and Bradford's strategy proved to be at least partially correct: the Port accepted EDA's conditions. But whether it accepted the conditions as wholeheartedly as it accepted the funds remained to be seen.

By the time of the April 29 announcement, a three-way agreement between the EDA, the port, and World Airways had been forged as a precondition for the start of a $10 million hangar project. The EDA would make a grant and loan to the port for building the hangar; World Airways would lease the facility for forty years for a rent that would cover the port's financing and other costs and increase with its earnings there. Finally, as part of the lease's conditions, President Ed Daly of World would agree with the EDA on an employment plan to provide jobs for unemployed Oakland residents, who would be trained at government expense to qualify for them.[42]

From the beginning, the success of the EDA program depended on agreement among a diverse group of participants with differing organizational objectives. The port and World Airways saw federal funds as an aid in increasing their capital facilities, while the EDA Oakland task force was primarily interested in the rapid development of jobs for unemployed minorities. Even within the EDA there were disagreements between advocates of the employment plan and those who felt that enforcement of the plan would make rapid completion of the projects more difficult.

To recapitulate, Foley declared in the April 29 announcement that the EDA had agreed to offer public works grants and loans totaling $23,289,000; 60 percent of the total would be grants and 40 percent would be loans. The projects were: airport hangar, $10,650,-000 (to Port of Oakland; to be leased by World Airways); marine terminal, $10,125,000 (to Port of Oakland); port industrial park, $2,100,000 (to Port of Oakland); and access road to coliseum, $414,-000 (to city of Oakland). Other public works projects were awarded to the Port of Oakland at later dates. They included: air cargo terminal, $184,000 (approved February 1, 1966); twenty small aircraft hangers, $76,000 (approved June 15, 1966); and auxiliary airport tower, $223,000 (approved February 1, 1967).[43]

42. *Ibid.,* p. 160.
43. Source of figures: Resnikoff, p. 37.

## SPRING AND SUMMER: FLESHING OUT THE EDA PROGRAM

The EDA program began to take shape in the spring and summer of 1966. Amory Bradford initiated employment plan discussions with World Airways in May, and in June Mayor Reading organized a series of seminars to acquaint local businessmen with all federal loan programs.

EDA officials were still worried about the city's ability to develop an overall economic development plan; the first plan, done by Stanford Research Institute, was criticized by EDA officials as "providing inadequate directions as to what to do in Oakland's economy." Also, the EDA was skeptical about the city's ability to form a "broad-based committee" to monitor and amend such a plan. In an effort to find out more about Oakland's economy and politics, and to try to identify a group of people who might offer support to its program, the EDA in July awarded Floyd Hunter a $400,000 contract to make an "economic power structure" study of the city and to evaluate certain ongoing programs. From the beginning, EDA officials were unclear about what an overall development plan was, why such a plan was needed, and how a power structure study was related to the plan.

On October 5 the Oakland program suffered a severe jolt when Eugene Foley announced his resignation as head of the EDA. In a later interview, Foley said he quit "because I could see the way the wind was blowing. Commerce was cracking down on EDA—the White House had decided that EDA should not be spending money in cities. Vietnam was eating everything up." Although the Oakland team was surprised and depressed by Foley's departure, there were hopeful developments in Oakland that kept alive a spirit of optimism. By the end of the summer, an eight-member Employment Plan Review Board had been formed, with one representative from each of the five poverty target areas and one each from labor, management, and the EDA.[44]

44. The labor representative, Norman Amundsen, had been selected directly by the Alameda County Central Labor Council; representing management was Ken Thompson, who had talked to EDA officials on a number of occasions since the Dunsmuir meetings. Cesar Flores Mendez, a businessman, was appointed by the "Spanish-speaking" target area committee. The members from each of the other target areas were black housewives: Mrs. Ruby

The first meeting, to organize the committee, was held on September 8. At the next meeting, on October 8, the committee reviewed the Employment Plans of three Oakland applicants for business loans. (We will discuss the experience of this program in chapter 4). Bennie's Candies, Rainbow Car Wash, and Colombo Bakeries were all successful before the committee. (Bennie would receive a loan of $64,000 which he said would help him create 25 jobs. Rainbow would obtain $135,000 for a projected 35 jobs; Colombo would receive $423,000 for a projected job increase of 158.)[45]

At its third meeting on November 12, the board approved two additional employment plans. The first was based on a business loan of $241,000 to Sierra Cotton Mills, which planned to add sixty-six new employees over a two-year period and to provide on-the-job training. The second employment plan presented at the meeting was that of World Airways. After projecting a list of "Additional Personnel to be Hired, 1967–1971," the World employment plan stated that "World and the appropriate governmental agencies undertake to make training opportunities available to the fullest extent possible to unemployed and under-employed residents of Oakland."[46] (By October it had been agreed that World Airways would set up and operate a training program, with the government paying the cost. The program would be funded under Section 241 of the Manpower Development and Training Act, which provided support for programs in EDA-designated areas. EDA officials had decided against locating the training program at the East Bay Skills Center, "partly because it would be better to locate it at the airport, but more because the Skills Center was still suffering from administrative confusion."[47] The training program had always been regarded by EDA officials as a critical ingredient in the capacity of the hangar project to create jobs.)

World Airways further promised to use realistic tests in recruiting for the training programs, in an effort to "avoid the cultural bias found in many existing tests or qualifications." Finally, the plan

---

Baker, West Oakland; Mrs. Jewel Manley, North Oakland; Mrs. Willie Thompson, Fruitvale; and Mrs. Marjorie Woods, East Oakland.

45. For a more detailed account of this meeting, see Resnikoff, pp. 25–27.

46. Employment Plan of World Air Center, Inc. and World Airways, Inc., approved by the EDA on December 14, 1966.

47. Bradford, p. 162.

stated that "preference will be given to qualified residents of the city of Oakland in the filling of positions resulting from the expansion of operations" by World.

The plan recognized fully that predicting future events is an uncertain enterprise: "This Plan is based upon the method and scope of operation now contemplated by World in the hangar which is to be constructed at the Port of Oakland. If World's method and scope of operation is changed, World shall have the right to amend this Plan consistent with its stated objectives, . . . subject to EDA approval." And again:

World and EDA recognize the extreme complexity of predicting business expansion, designing new training programs which will meet FAA standards, developing instructional and institutional forms which will allow previously unskilled and unemployed Oakland residents to move rapidly into highly skilled positions in a growing industry, and assuming that these persons will be sufficiently trained and qualified to take responsibility for the lives of air travelers utilizing World's services.

Even with these conditioning paragraphs, the plan seemed hopeful enough to the review board, which approved it at the November 12 meeting.

That meeting was the last appearance of Amory Bradford as an EDA consultant. He wrote in his book that "Approval of the World Airways Plan, by a Board that had learned to function well, rounded out all that I had set out to do when I began in Oakland in January, nine months earlier. It was time to go."[48] In Washington, Bradford gave a detailed briefing on Oakland to Ross Davis, who had succeeded Foley as head of the EDA.

As 1966 came to an end, there were unmistakable stirrings of activity in Oakland. Mayor Reading had sponsored a job fair in September to bring job developers and job seekers together. (An EDA technical assistance grant had helped the city to cover the small deficit incurred.) Then the mayor moved to establish a manpower commission that would support job training and placement efforts in the city. On December 14 the EDA and World Airways formally signed the employment plan agreement, which promised to create a significant supply of new jobs.

Some difficulties did develop in the EDA program in the last half of 1966, but for the most part they appeared to be "technical" ones

48. *Ibid.*, p. 169.

that did not raise fundamental questions of discrimination or willingness to hire the unemployed. During the summer, an EDA consultant had objected to the method by which the port was filling the area to be used for the marine terminal. In the consultant's opinion, the material being used for filling the bay—material that came from Bay Area Rapid Transit construction sites—contained a great amount of objectionable debris.[49] Because of this, and because the EDA determined that the proposed tenant of that area, Matson Navigation Company, would not provide sizable new employment, the port decided to move the EDA-financed project to a different area. (The Matson Company, frankly admitting that it did not plan extensive new hiring, had requested to be separated from the port's arrangement with the EDA.)

There were also disputes in 1966 between the EDA and the port over reimbursement of in-house engineering expenses and the method of disbursement of federal funds. But these, once again, appeared to be technical issues that could be worked out.

What seemed important was that the EDA had made a substantial financial commitment to Oakland and that that commitment was tied to the creation of jobs for the hard-core unemployed. Foley, Bradford, and the task force had supplied the initial push that had attracted nationwide publicity; now all that remained was the carrying out of the plans.

49. EDA project progress report, April 10, 1968.

# 3

## Trials of Implementation

THE ROAD OF PROJECT EXECUTION, 1966–1968

Although EDA officials had thought that designing the innovative policy, committing funds, and obtaining initial local agreements were the most crucial parts of the program, the implementation of the program proved surprisingly difficult. This chapter will show how the "technical details" of implementation, which had not initially been a source of concern, combined to delay the program and frustrate its sponsors' hopes.

IMPLEMENTATION: MARINE TERMINAL

Before construction of the 7th Street Marine Terminal could begin, a number of thorny issues had to be resolved. One of these issues was the quality of filling material that the port was planning to put in San Francisco Bay. After a summer of dispute on the matter in 1966, Walter Butler (the EDA's consultant) conducted an investigation and found that "practices not always conducive to sound engineering have persisted on the filling portion of this project. Debris, garbage, timber, etc. have found their way into the Terminal area fill. The project generally seems to have suffered from lack of co-ordinated planning."[1] Butler also found that the structural stability of

1. Letter from Walter Butler to Henry Brooks, chief EDA Public Works engineer, September 2, 1966.

the dikes was "marginal." Throughout the last half of 1966, the port and the EDA continued to disagree about the quality of bay fill.

Another subject of dispute concerned advance funding. On June 17, 1966, Ben Nutter, executive director of the port, had written to Foley requesting that the port be reimbursed for " 'in house' engineering expenses where, for small items and under urgency conditions, the Port staff is available to do the work."[2] (In order to expedite the application, the port had used its own staff for preliminary engineering work.)

On July 15, 1966, J. Monroe Sullivan of the port wrote to the EDA about a troubling provision of the Oakland city charter that would make the port dependent on advance funding from the federal government. A section of the charter had been interpreted to mean that the port might raise money by issuing revenue bonds and by issuing certificates of indebtedness. In effect, said Sullivan, this prohibited the port from borrowing money unless there was a pledge of revenues from the facility involved. And in this case, the port had pledged revenues from the industrial park (and surplus revenues from the hangar and marine facilities) to the EDA. Because the charter made it difficult for the port to borrow money for work on these projects, Sullivan wrote, "our goal . . . is to make sure that the interim financing is available out of EDA funds when it is needed."[3]

Difficulties concerning interim financing were causing delays in the project. The EDA's general policy is never to advance grant funds for interim development and construction financing. On a few occasions loans have been advanced to some applicants, usually Indian reservations, who were unable to obtain interim financing on their own. But in normal cases, the applicants must secure their own interim financing. The EDA includes the interest on the grantee's borrowed interim financing as part of the legitimate project cost. (The strict policy on interim financing is designed both to encourage the recipients' initiative in raising money and to protect the EDA from spending money for a project that might never be completed.) On July 18 an EDA representative held a discouraging meeting with port officials where he was told "that no work was in progress on any of the projects, as no plans, specifications, contract docu-

2. Letter from Nutter to Foley, June 17, 1966.
3. Letter from Sullivan to Jack Beddow, EDA Office of General Counsel, July 15, 1966.

ments were available. The Port does not have sufficient funds to contract with A/E [architect/engineer] for preparation of same."[4] Federal policy and local requests could not easily be reconciled. Ross Davis, the EDA administrator who was later to take over direction of the agency, wrote a sharp reply to the port commissioners on July 19. Based on federal regulations, Davis said, "It is EDA policy not to disburse any Federal funds until contracts have been awarded for an entire project. . . . We have previously stated to you, and your staff, the fact that reimbursement for in-house engineering or other functions performed by your regular staff is not an authorized project cost item."[5]

Still, the port continued to press its claims. At an August 31 conference in Oakland, the port proposed that EDA deposit grant/loan funds in a special joint account to pay authorized construction and administrative costs based on a quarterly estimate of construction placement and other project expenses. The EDA replied to the port proposal by telegram on September 9:

WE DO NOT BELIEVE THAT SUCH AN ARRANGEMENT CAN BE JUSTIFIED OR IS CONSISTENT WITH ESTAB. GOVT. CONTRACTING POLICY. HOWEVER, DUE TO THE REQUIREMENTS OF THE OAKLAND PROJECTS AND TO THE REQUIREMENTS OF THE CITY CHARTER, WE WILL CONSIDER A MONTHLY DISBURSEMENT OF FUNDS, ONCE ALL CONTRACTS FOR EACH PROJECT HAVE BEEN LET. . . .[6]

No advances of federal funds would be forthcoming, but approved construction costs incurred by the port for a particular month could be covered by the EDA after the month was over. Furthermore, loan (not grant) funds would be advanced to the port for architect and engineering services.

Now, it seemed, the terminal project could go on. But other difficulties remained: the soils dispute continued through October, and Matson Navigation Company (the prospective tenant of the terminal) stated that it would be unable to provide sufficient new employment. (Matson had also been far from enthusiastic about the EDA's employment plan idea.) For these reasons, the port decided to bypass

4. Memo from Walter F. Rasp, EDA engineer, to Orrin Fayle, chief of construction management, Office of Public Works, July 18, 1966.

5. Letter from Ross D. Davis to port commissioners, July 19, 1966.

6. Telegram from Orrin Fayle, EDA, to Ben Nutter, Port of Oakland, September 9, 1966.

both the soils and Matson problems by moving the EDA-financed project to the western end of the diked construction area.

No further action was taken until late January 1967, when the port submitted an application to relocate the EDA project. This time, the project included a glass tourist-type restaurant. On April 12, 1967 the EDA approved the change in project location; two days later, the port submitted its architecture/engineering (A/E) agreement to the EDA. The federal agency approved the agreement on June 25. But once again progress was slow. A subsequent EDA report noted that, after approval of the A/E contract, "the Engineer did not start on the work for several months because his forces were busy on other work for the Port of Oakland."[7] Not until the fall of 1967 did the architect/engineer start work.

In November 1967 other kinds of problems were developing. Cliff Holden, an engineer who had become the EDA project manager in Oakland, wrote in a memo:

I had a call from Mr. Champ Corsen of the Naval Facilities Engineering Command, San Bruno, today. . . . He read me some correspondence that had been going on between the Port of Oakland and the Navy in regard to serious navigational hazards caused by construction of this project. This is a matter that the Port has never told the EDA about. . . . When the existing dike was built the pattern of the currents in the entrance channel to the Naval Supply Center was changed. . . . It is difficult for ships to navigate.[8]

The military would be heard from again.

On January 17, 1968, the port requested that the terminal project be broken into two phases, which included dredging and filling as phase 1 and construction of the remainder of the terminal as phase 2. The port also requested a $2,000,000 loan advance to finance phase 1.[9] On January 30 EDA Oakland recommended to Washington that the January 17 letter from the port be approved. But on February 6 John Davidson of the EDA Western Area Office in Seattle sent a letter to George Karras in Washington objecting to the Oakland office's memo. By the next day, the Public Works Office in Seattle had agreed to support the port's letter of January 17, provided they

7. EDA project progress report, April 10, 1968.
8. Memo from Cliff Holden to Western Area Office, November 22, 1967.

9. The 1967 and 1968 sections of the marine terminal chronology are based in part on a memo written in December 1968 by Frederick A. Ricci, who was an EDA staff member in Oakland at that time.

were given a resolution by the port commissioners in which the board agreed to build the restaurant at a later date if enough funds were not available at the time for opening the bids. In response the port passed such a resolution on February 20, and on February 21 the Western Area Office threw its suport behind the loan advance. Washington responded favorably.

At this point, the Navy reentered the story to add an additional protest to the terminal project. On April 1, 1968, Rear Admiral F. E. Janney, director of the Shore Installations Division, wrote a strong letter to the EDA's Office of Public Works. During the previous year, the navy had objected to the terminal project because of its effects on ship navigation. Now the issue was airplane safety. Admiral Janney declared that "the Navy is seriously concerned over the possible adverse effects that construction of the proposed Port of Oakland pier extension and associated equipment would have on the flight safety and operational capability of Naval Air Station, Alameda. Of particular concern are the mobile crane at the western end of the new pier and the masts of ships which may be berthed at the pier."[10] The matter was pending before the Federal Aviation Administration, and all sides waited eagerly for that body to rule. Meanwhile, the Port of Oakland had requested another change of plans. On April 7, 1968, the port submitted a plan to construct a larger, revolving resturant at a cost of over $1,000,000 and to eliminate the south wharf and transit sheds. The public works officer at the EDA's Western Area Office replied on May 20 that his office felt that the elimination of the south wharf was a "major change in scope." Therefore, on May 31 the Western Area Office sent a letter to the Port of Oakland stating that the letter of April 7 constituted a "major revision" and that a new project application would have to be submitted for approval by EDA head Ross Davis. The port answered the Western Area Office on May 31 by saying that it only wanted to use $630,-000 of project funds for a restaurant. This was the amount of money available after a crane was eliminated because of the navy objections.

While controversy swirled around the design of the terminal, progress was being made on preparations for dredging and filling. The port submitted plans for dredging and filling to the EDA on

10. Letter from Admiral Janney to Frank A. Cirillo, Office of Public Works, April 1, 1968.

April 29, 1968. Bids for this part of the project were advertised on July 15, but on August 19 all bids were returned unopened because the port could not get a dredging permit from the Army Corps of Engineers. (A disagreement between the Bay Area Rapid Transit District (BARTD) and the port was the reason for the delay in corps approval; BARTD had charged that the dredging for the 7th Street terminal was too close to its dikes in the bay.)

As the summer of 1968 wore on and the disagreement between the port and the Western Area Office concerning the proposed change in plans remained unresolved, other complications arose. On August 1 the United States General Accounting Office (GAO) questioned the EDA's awards to the Port of Oakland on the basis that the 60–40 grant/loan ratio might be too generous. The GAO felt that the port was strong enough to get funds elsewhere, but the EDA replied that other factors—like the special needs of the area—justified the port contracts.[11] Later that month the San Francisco Department of Public Works complained that the port's dumping could affect water contact sports in the bay.[12]

As 1968 ended and a new administration prepared to come to power in Washington, the future plans for the terminal lay in doubt. In the areas of dredging, filling, financing, design, and relationships with other governmental institutions, the technical problems surrounding construction of the marine terminal had proved to be formidable. What had appeared initially to be a relatively straightforward program now involved new and unforeseen participants—the navy, the GAO, local government bodies—whose agreement was necessary if the program was to continue.

IMPLEMENTATION: WORLD AIRWAYS HANGAR

Progress on the marine terminal, although beset by numerous problems, was actually smooth compared to the evils that affected the other major public works project—the aircraft maintenance hangar. Although the hangar project had been approved on April 29, 1966, no action was taken for several months while the port negotiated a lease with the proposed tenant (World Airways) and the

11. EDA report of meeting with GAO, August 1, 1968.
12. Letter from San Francisco Department of Public Works to U.S. Army Corps of Engineers, August 19, 1968.

employment plan was prepared and accepted. The architect/engineering agreement was submitted to the EDA on February 6, 1967, and approved March 6. On May 6 the port entered into a contract with Charles Luckman and Associates (an architecture/engineering firm). But not until August 14, 1967, did the port notify the Luckman firm to start work.

Opinions differed over the reason the A/E did not begin work sooner. "There is no apparent reason for this delay," an EDA progress report stated in April 1968, "other than the fact that the Port spent some time going through the process of requesting and receiving an advance on the project loan to finance drawings which were revised to meet the requirements of World Airways."[13] Ben Nutter, executive director of the port, offered another interpretation of the delay. After the port had signed the contract with Luckman in May, World Airways had retained Luckman to develop industrial engineering information for a general building program. According to Nutter, this study would outline specific project criteria for designing the hangar, and the building program was not received until August 1967, causing the delay.[14]

When Charles Luckman and Associates had completed an initial plan on April 2, 1968, they had some bad news for both the port and the EDA. John R. Campbell of the A/E firm notified Ben Nutter that there were some increased construction costs.[15] The construction cost for the hangar in 1966 had been estimated at $9,262,600. Now the figure had leaped to $13,425,840; thus, the total construction cost increase was $4,163,240. The Luckman representative enumerated the reasons for the cost increase:

*(1) Building Cost Escalation of 13.5 percent.*—There had been a time lapse caused by discussions with the EDA about the manner of funding. The preparation of the World Airways building program had taken time. Cost increase, $1,250,451.

*(2) Fire Protection Requirements.*—Insurance companies had complained that the port's original plans for the hangar did not include sufficient protection against fires. The necessary requirements were defined by the insurance carriers. Cost increase, $866,000.

13. EDA project progress report, April 10, 1968.
14. Letter from Nutter to Lambert O'Malley, EDA Public Works, April 2, 1968.
15. Letter from John R. Campbell to Nutter, April 2, 1968.

*(3) Improvements.*—As the result of the building program and subsequent decisions by World Airways, the configuration of office areas was changed and there was an increase in utilities. Cost Increase, $889,762.

*(4) Aircraft Requirements.*—Fences were added to the later plan, along with improved paving for heavier planes. Cost increase, $1,-157,027.

Immediately after receiving the new estimates from the Luckman firm, Ben Nutter wrote to Lambert O'Malley (then the EDA's public works director) to tell him about the changes.[16] It could not have been pleasant reading for the EDA:

|  | *1966* | *1968* |
|---|---|---|
| Cost of construction (estimated) | 9,262,600 | 13,425,840 |
| Total project cost (estimated) | 10,650,000 | 15,196,520 |

After disclosing the new figures, Nutter had a request to make: "We respectfully request that EDA consider making available the additional funds required to complete this project, as outlined in the . . . estimate of project cost as revised April 2, 1968." On May 27 the port submitted an application to the EDA for an additional assistance grant of $2,214,000, which would provide financing for approximately half of the overrun estimated at that time. The port later explained that it would finance the other half of the hangar overrun by issuing revenue bonds on the open market.[17]

For the next few months, the port and the EDA argued about engineering considerations lying behind the increased costs. At a July 26 meeting in Oakland, EDA officials asked why the roof of the hangar had to be eighty-five feet high. They were told that this height was required to remove and work on the tail section of the new 747 airplanes.[18]

By August 30 EDA regional officials had come out in favor of the port's request for additional assistance, provided "that the employment plan of World Airways and the training programs that it necessitates will assure that members of the hard-core poverty group in Oakland will be trained and hired."[19] On September 13 an optimistic

16. Letter from Nutter to O'Malley, April 2, 1968.
17. See letter from Nutter to Valmer Cameron, EDA Western Area Office director, June 17, 1968.
18. EDA memo on meeting of July 26, 1968.
19. Memo from Davidson to Bill Rae, Western Area Office, August 30, 1968.

Davidson wrote that Charles Patterson, the Oakland representative, "has assured me that the employment plans were satisfactorily solved and that we can now send the overrun recommendation to Washington."[20] Patterson added on September 17 that World's "efforts to meet its requirements under the Employment Plan" were "consistent with EDA's expectations."[21]

EDA officials in Washington, D.C., were much less enthusiastic at this time about World Airways' employment performance than were their counterparts in the field. A World Airways compliance report of June 1968 had indicated that, while total employment at World Airways had increased by 98 employees (from 1004 in March 1967 to 1102 in February 1968), the total number of minority employees dropped from 129 to 111.[22]

The internal report on Oakland completed by the Urban Affairs Division of the EDA in October 1968 recommended that any increased financial assistance for the hangar should be conditioned on approval of a revised, stronger employment plan for World Airways. (Provision for renegotiation of the plan in the case of a "change of circumstances" was contained in the original employment plan agreement. The alterations on hangar design and costs were felt by the report to constitute such a change.) A revised plan would include (a) the delineation of employment categories with explicit job qualification requirements; and commitments from World Airways (b) to employ graduates of the East Bay Skills Center, an existing training program, and (c) to support the development of training programs and to make available on-the-job training for positions requiring less than EDA or federal contract compliance certification.[23]

The report stated that the "EDA should attempt to extract these commitments from World Airways without agreeing to any additional financial assistance,"[24] but the writers of the report recognized that this might be difficult. Additional money might be useful as a bargaining counter. (In this case, the bargaining was somewhat complicated. The port, which was in charge of building the hangar,

20. Davidson memo, September 13, 1968.

21. Letter from Charles J. Patterson to Russell Stevens, area attorney, September 17, 1968.

22. Compliance Report ED-613, cited in letter from Ross Davis to Robert Mortensen, president, Board of Port Commissioners, February 26, 1969.

23. EDA internal report, p. 79.

24. *Ibid.,* p. 80.

had asked for additional funding. The EDA would be trying to use its control over this funding to force concessions from World Airways, the lessee and future beneficiary of the hangar. Attempting to control funding for one institution to force changes in the behavior of another would prove to be an exasperatingly indirect process.)

Even if the EDA did decide to grant the overrun request and to use it as a bargaining counter, there were a number of shapes such a decision might take. The report outlined some of the alternatives for EDA: (1) approve the overrun request in a 60–40 grant/loan ratio; (2) in line with GAO complaints, reduce the grant ratio to 56.3 percent for supplemental grants to *all* of the Oakland projects, including the hangar; (3) reduce the grant/loan ratio to 50 percent on the hangar project. Of course the EDA had other alternatives: (4) deny the overrun request; or even (5) withdraw support completely from the hangar project.

Noting the small rate of progress in both construction and job creation, the internal report pointed out that the EDA could withdraw on any of the following conditions of the original loan and grant agreement: finding that representations in the application were incorrect or incomplete in any material respect; determining that the borrower has failed to proceed with reasonable diligence in the financing or construction of the project; or determining that the scope or character of the project has changed substantially so as to adversely affect accomplishment of the project as intended.[25] The report suggested that, in the case of the hangar, the EDA might be able to justify the complete termination of the project.

On December 18, 1968, George Karras and Louis Phillips (of the EDA's Office of Policy Coordination) met with members of the port's staff in Oakland to discuss the hangar project. At the meeting Karras and Phillips outlined the EDA's concern about the project's progress and the realization of the goal of creating jobs for the hard-core unemployed and underemployed residents of Oakland.[26] In response to the EDA's questions, the port and World Airways sent letters to Karras that discussed employment and training activities. Both letters were dated December 31. Ben Nutter emphasized the port's commitment to the Oakland minority community. Edward J.

25. *Ibid.*, p. 71.
26. Noted in the EDA Oakland file, compiled August 15, 1969.

Daly, president of World Airways, sent an enclosure entitled "Developing Jobs for the Unemployed and Underemployed: Affirmative Action by World Airways, Inc." This pamphlet described World's role in helping to establish FIPCO and Sons, Inc., a black-owned and black-managed corporation that would service and clean aircraft. Furthermore, the enclosure stated that World's president was serving as Oakland metropolitan chairman of the National Alliance of Businessmen and that World was active in the JOBS program. Also, World had cooperated with the Urban Coalition in contracting with a black-managed firm to produce slipper socks for use on World's commercial charter flights. Finally, World had supported the Opportunities Industrialization Center (the black-directed training program started by Leon Sullivan) in its operations in Oakland.

Still, Washington EDA officials were skeptical. At the end of 1968 they were considering the bleak alternatives open to them on the hangar project. If they approved funding for the overrun, the EDA would be still further committed to the project and there would be no guarantee that costs would not rise again. If they denied the overrun, the whole project would be in stalemate. If they canceled the hangar project completely, the money that had been allocated would revert to the federal treasury. The project appeared to be bogged down in a quagmire from which there was no promising exit.

IMPLEMENTATION: TRAINING PROGRAM

In the eyes of EDA officials, the hangar project could only produce jobs for the unemployed if it were linked to an effective training program for those who would work at the hangar. In October 1966 it had been agreed that World Airways would set up and operate a government-funded training program for airline maintenance personnel. The program would be set up under Section 241 of the Manpower Development and Training Act (MDTA), which provides funds for EDA-designated areas.

Although the idea of job training sounds straightforward, the process under Section 241 of the MDTA is incredibly convoluted. Opportunities for delay or termination of a proposal are present at many points along the way. This is how the process works: First, the group proposing a training program must demonstrate that there is a need for employees in a certain type of industry. The relevant state's department of employment must conduct a survey of the industry in order to evaluate the need. If such a need is proved, the proposal goes to the local MDTA advisory committee, which is composed of representatives of management, labor, and minority groups. That committee must approve the proposal, and the department of vocational education of the state must certify that the proposed training institution is acceptable. Then the proposal must go to the chief elected official of the political subdivision for his approval (in this case, the mayor of Oakland).

Following local approval, the MDTA proposal travels to the state capital, where the state's department of employment and department of vocational education must approve it. (The department of employment is a delegate agency for the U.S. Department of Labor; the department of vocational education is delegate agency for the U.S. Department of Health, Education, and Welfare. Because Section 241 of the MDTA requires joint approval by the EDA *and* the federal Departments of Labor and HEW, the process is further complicated.)

From the state capital, the proposal goes to the federal regional offices of Labor and HEW. (In this case, the regional offices are located in San Francisco.) Then the proposal is sent to Washington, where it must be approved by the EDA and the departments of Labor and HEW.[27] Federal officials who were interested in 1970 were quick to point out that the EDA does not have direct control over Section 241 funds; it must secure the approval of Labor and HEW for any training program under this section.

In the case of the World Airways training proposal, the MDTA Advisory Council in Oakland approved a plan on November 30, 1966, that would train 510 aircraft maintenance personnel. On March 13, 1967, Norman Amundson, chairman of the council, wrote to Alexander Trowbridge, acting secretary of commerce, to ask what had happened to the proposal.[28] Trowbridge turned the letter over to Ross Davis of the EDA, who wrote Amundson, "We are aware that such a proposal is being developed. . . . This project is still in Cali-

27. We are indebted to Hugh Taylor of the EDA for helping us to understand this difficult procedure.
28. Letter from Norman Amundson to Alexander Trowbridge, March 13, 1967.

fornia; when it arrives in Washington it will . . . be given prompt consideration by the Interagency Review Committee."[29]

A copy of Davis' letter was forwarded to Albert Tieburg of the California Department of Employment; Tieburg then explained to Davis that the proposal had been sent by his office to the state Department of Education four months earlier. The state employment official said he hoped "that the necessary work on these proposals will be completed in the very near future so that they may be forwarded for funding."[30] In May 1967 an *Oakland Tribune* article featured Amundson's charges that "Red tape and inter-agency jealousies are delaying critically-needed job training for Alameda County's unemployed."[31]

When the training proposal finally reached Washington, it proved impossible for the EDA, Labor, and HEW to agree jointly to support it. The EDA was worried about the costs per trainee; HEW felt it would be too much of a financial opportunity for World. Later, the Manpower Development and Training Act was amended to give statutory preference to established skills centers in the competition for federal MDTA funds. Because the East Bay Skills Center was on the HEW list of established skills centers, HEW would have a powerful argument against a separate training center for World. Success in HEW's terms meant training and finding jobs for poor people, and conducting that process through skills centers. A rival training institution would necessarily diminish the number of possible placements.

Although federal officials vary somewhat in their interpretations of how the training proposal was killed, by 1968 it was clear that the three federal agencies could not get together to approve the project. Finally, World Airways withdrew its proposal. A key part of the EDA Oakland project had been dismantled. Like the construction of public works projects, the creation of a training program eventually required a long string of clearances by actors with different perspectives. Although the EDA wanted to set up a separate training school for airline mechanics, HEW defined success in terms of en-

29. Letter from Ross Davis to Norman Amundson, March 28, 1967.
30. Letter from Albert Tieburg to Ross Davis, April 21, 1967.
31. "Expert Raps Delay in Job Program," *Oakland Tribune,* May 14, 1967, p. 5.

hancing established skills centers. Given these divergent organizational objectives, the building of agreement—which was necessary for the furtherance of the program—became a difficult task.

While EDA projects in Oakland were running into local difficulties of engineering and financing, it became clear that the federal agency itself was becoming less interested in Oakland. "The departure of Foley in the Fall of 1966," the agency's internal report declares, "followed shortly thereafter by a number of key staff people who had helped run the program in its first year, marked a dramatic shift in the emphasis of the Oakland program. . . . When the Oakland program was placed in normal agency channels in Washington, its priority and singular importance diminished."[32]

After 1966 Oakland ceased to be the favored project of the EDA. A number of reasons are given for this: resentment of the task force by senior staff members whose channels had been bypassed; disapproval of the project by the secretary of commerce and the White House; overidentification of the project with Eugene Foley personally. Ross Davis, who succeeded Foley, feels that it is a mistake to expect the federal agency to be a constant initiator of action: "Of course, from Washington it seemed that nothing in Oakland was moving for much of 1967 and 1968. And I was worried. But tradition has it that it was the locals who were supposed to move things, not the feds."[33]

When Amory Bradford left Oakland in November 1966, Doug Costle took over the operation of the local EDA office on an interim basis. Costle devoted much of his time to the development of an interagency Federal Executive Board (FEB) task force, which would examine the federal delivery system in Oakland. The FEB task force idea had originated in the EDA. During 1966 that agency had encouraged other federal departments to participate in and contribute financially to the study and they had done so.

Costle left the EDA in January 1967, and the permanent operation of the Oakland office was taken over by Charles Patterson, a

32. EDA internal report, pp. 51–52.
33. Interview with Ross Davis, July 17, 1970.

black ex-Peace Corps official. The EDA internal report contrasts Amory Bradford's conception of his role in Oakland—"negotiation, discussion, and dialogue with all segments of the community"—with Patterson's decision "not to spend his time negotiating with black militants and other target area residents because of his conviction that there was nothing left which EDA could promise or deliver."[34] The report notes that Patterson devoted much of his time to the chairmanship of the FEB task force (which produced a published report in August 1968), and it records his view that "the publicity given the EDA program raised the expectations of the people in the Oakland ghetto far beyond EDA's capacity to deliver."[35] With promises already made and the difficulties of implementation increasing, Patterson felt his position growing increasingly difficult.

In Washington Ross Davis responded to Patterson's difficulties by making some administrative changes: "Patterson had the advantage of being black. I thought that would help him, but Patterson wasn't enough. So I appointed an ad hoc group in Washington in the first half of 1967 to keep in touch with Patterson. I really had great confidence in Patterson, but after a year, it became apparent that things were not moving."[36] A succession of EDA staff men—Michael Coleman, Blair Butterworth, and Fred Ricci—were sent to Oakland to back up Patterson in the office. And Davis asked Jonathan Lindley, deputy assistant secretary for policy coordination, to do an evaluation of the entire Oakland project (which resulted in the internal report).

What finally created a sense of urgency in Washington regarding the Oakland project was the port's request in mid-1968 for an overrun on the airplane hangar. "That," says Ross Davis, "perforce brought our attention back to Oakland."

Washington, D.C., and Oakland were not the only places where administrative difficulties occurred during 1967 and 1968; the role of the Western Area Office in Seattle constituted perhaps the biggest question mark of all. Technical assistance programs were handled directly between Washington and Oakland, but Seattle was charged with "limited program authority" in the public works and fully dis-

34. EDA internal report, p. 56.
35. *Ibid.*
36. Ross Davis interview.

bursed business loans projects.[37] Although the area office did not have the authority to approve or deny funding requests, it was supposed to facilitate "project management."

In a series of memos to Washington, D.C., the Seattle office searched for a definition of its role. On December 15, 1966, for example, John Davidson of the area office wrote: "This memo is for the purpose of (1) providing data to the project files in the WAO and in Washington D.C., (2) to indicate Area Office understanding of who is handling the project, (3) to request closer coordination between headquarters and the Western Area Office in work assignments to consultants."[38] Davidson's complaint was that "WAO had not been informed about the assignment of a consultant to the project." Walter Butler Company had been retained by the Washington office to do a further study of the terminal project, and Davidson felt that Seattle should have been in on the decision.

The response in Washington was not sympathetic to the regional official. Chief Public Works Engineer Henry Brooks wrote a memo to George Karras:

We find no data or comment from the Western Area Office which might be helpful in evaluating the proposed revised project. . . . It is difficult to understand why Mr. Davidson did not know Walter Butler was serving as consultant on this project. . . . Mr. Davidson has raised this question several times and each time it has been explained to him that when a consultant has previously been employed to assist in a project, we have felt it wise to continue the relationship to avoid confusion and maintain some consistency in relation to the projects.[39]

In a later memo to Karras, Brooks was even more blunt: "I hate to waste your time and my time on this trivial complaint by John Davidson, but I feel somehow he must understand our operations here."[40]

A continual concern of the area office was the nature of the "special relationship" between Washington and Oakland. In February 1968 Davidson wrote to Karras that he had talked with Patterson and the two had agreed that:

(1) The Oakland office would send all construction management matters to the WAO through Mr. Holden, Project Manager

37. EDA internal report, p. 52.
38. Memo from Davidson to Washington EDA, December 15, 1966.
39. Memo from Brooks to Karras, December 22, 1966.
40. Memo from Brooks to Karras, December 27, 1966.

(2) At any time that Mr. Patterson has a special concern about a project matter, particularly with regard to policy or the need for a rapid decision, he will make his recommendations directly to the Area Office.[41]

To the present time, the role of the Western Area Office remains unresolved.

Charles Patterson resigned from the EDA in December 1968 to take a position as vice-president of World Airways. He was replaced by Hugh Taylor, an employment expert who had served at the East Bay Skills Center and as director of Mayor Reading's Manpower Commission. The position into which Taylor now stepped was not an enviable one: Washington's attitude toward the Oakland program was unclear; implementation of the projects themselves was moving slowly, if at all; and the Western Area Office in Seattle was asking for greater authority over Oakland. Thus, within the EDA itself, organizational units had differing perspectives with respect to the Oakland projects.

### EDA RECEIVES—BUT DOES NOT ACCEPT—
### THE POWER STRUCTURE STUDY

One area of continuing disappointment to the EDA was its attempt to discover a decision-making apparatus in Oakland that could throw its weight behind federal projects. In the summer of 1968, Floyd Hunter presented the federal agency with his power structure study of Oakland. But Hunter's study—which included a defense of his power-structure methodology and a ranking of Oakland's most powerful decision makers—did not provide the EDA with the means of assembling a local force of allies. And federal officials were disturbed by the study's strong criticism of local officials. When the EDA asked Hunter to revise the study, the author refused. The agency then countered by threatening court action for nonfulfillment of contract unless the revisions were made.

### POLITICAL DEVELOPMENTS IN OAKLAND

When he left Oakland in the fall of 1966, Amory Bradford wrote a memo to Ross Davis that, among other things, described Bradford's impressions of Mayor John Reading's leadership:

The new Mayor, John Reading, . . . immediately accepted the major

41. Memo from Davidson to Karras, February 6, 1968.

premise of our program, the need to solve the problems of unemployment, by providing jobs, as his main goal. The announcement of our funded projects at the end of April gave him a good solid platform from which to launch his own efforts to mobilize the business community. He has taken full advantage of this, and we have worked closely and effectively with him. His activities have convinced the ghetto residents that he is trying, and that he cares about solving their problems. This has made all the difference.[42]

In January 1967, when Mayor Reading appointed his Manpower Commission, the EDA provided him with a technical assistance grant of $35,000 a year for two years to staff the commission. The EDA regarded the mayor as a prime asset.

But during 1967 and 1968 life became exceedingly difficult for Mayor Reading. The OEDC (community action agency) decided to declare its independence from the city in 1967; its militant new director, Percy Moore, advocated an aggressive kind of community organization that was hostile to City Hall. The model cities program which came to Oakland in 1968 appeared to be offering still more potential resources to groups in the black community who opposed the mayor. Also in 1968, a black boycott of downtown merchants over a police issue was denounced by the mayor.

Politics in Oakland were becoming more strident, more polarized, more hostile. The mayor, who had hoped to work with ghetto leaders in an atmosphere of rational persuasion, was deeply shaken. He could not understand the confrontation politics in which black leaders, searching for an opponent against whom to organize, repeatedly attacked the mayor as the leader of a reactionary city government. In fact, Reading had few resources with which to meet demands or punish enemies. And his troubles were not only with the black community. The federal government, to which the mayor turned for expanded assistance in the manpower field, repeatedly refused his requests. In the fall of 1968 Mayor Reading was withdrawing from active leadership and was strongly considering not running for re-election in 1969. The EDA was losing its supposed major asset of mayoral leadership.

DISAPPOINTING PROGRESS

In October 1968 the EDA took stock of its early group of public works projects (see Table 3). The results were a far cry from what

42. Memo from Bradford to Davis, October 21, 1966.

had been expected two years earlier. Not only had the two prime projects—marine terminal and aircraft hangar—failed to produce jobs; they were not even under construction. And the industrial park had managed to generate only about ten new jobs for Oakland residents.

Some progress was being made. The small hangars would be completed on December 3, 1968, and the air cargo terminal would be under construction a few months later. But overall, the EDA program looked disappointing, except for one public works project (the West Oakland Health Center) which we will discuss in chapter 4.

As 1968 drew to a close, the EDA program in Oakland was at a low ebb. Business loans had not resulted in many jobs, and public works projects were not even built. Delays were being caused by the difficulty of obtaining clearances on matters that had not been foreseen at the outset. And the general agreement on policy was dissolving into specific disagreements on the steps needed for implementation.

The major decision that now had to be made concerned the cost overrun on the airplane hangar. The project was the most expensive part of the Oakland program, and it had been expected to be the centerpiece of the whole experiment. The EDA's decision would not be long in coming.

### EDA SAYS "NO" (JANUARY-FEBRUARY 1969)

During Ross Davis' last months as head of the agency, in early 1969, the EDA's stance began to harden. On January 27 Davis wrote to the port commissioners, reiterating that the EDA's principal mission was to create job opportunities for the unemployed and underemployed.[43] Thus far, Davis said, the port and World Airways had not been sufficiently committed to this mission. "Before EDA can commit additional development resources in partnership with the Port of Oakland," he declared, "we should have adequate and detailed assurances that you intend and are able to carry out the objectives of our Oakland investment."[44]

Such assurances, Davis suggested, could be provided by an effective employment plan for the port itself and a revised plan for World

---

43. Letter from Ross Davis to port commissioners, January 27, 1969.
44. *Ibid.*

TABLE 3: Progress on Implementation Goes Slowly: The Status as of October 1968 of EDA Public Works Projects

| Project Title | Date Approved | Amount ($) | Under-/Over-run ($) | Status | Jobs Projected | Jobs to Date |
|---|---|---|---|---|---|---|
| Port of Oakland: 7th Street marine terminal | 4/29/66 | 10,125,000 | | Awaiting new design and impact projections | 175 plus indirect jobs | 0 |
| Port of Oakland: Block B industrial park | 4/29/66 | 2,100,000 | Underrun 490,000 | Completed October 1968 | 420 | Approximately 10 net new Oakland jobs* |
| Port of Oakland: aircraft maintenance hangar | 4/29/66 | 10,650,000 | Overrun 4,428,000 | Plans, financing under negotiation | 1,200 | 0 |
| Port of Oakland: 20 small aircraft hangars | 6/15/66 | 76,000 | | Under construction | 12 | 0 |
| Port of Oakland: air cargo terminal | 2/1/66 | 184,000 | | Plans and specifications under review | 12 | 0 |
| City of Oakland: four-lane access road | 4/29/66 | 414,000 | | Completed November 1966 | Indirect | — |
| Port of Oakland: auxiliary airport tower | 2/1/67 | 223,000 | | Design completed; will be constructed when main hangar is started | — | — |

*One firm located in area as of October 1968 was previously located in smaller quarters in Oakland.
Source: Resnikoff, "EDA in Oakland: An Evaluation." Figures from 1968 EDA report.

Airways. EDA staff would help the port and World devise acceptable plans. On January 31 Assistant Secretary Davis sent the port commissioners a set of guidelines that the EDA wanted to be incorporated into the new plans. The port was to pledge an on-the-job training program for minorities, and it was to promise to hire a "professional full-time Equal Employment Opportunity officer" to work with port tenants and encourage the hiring of minority unemployed. World Airways was to submit new employment projections and was also to promise to hire an equal employment opportunity officer.[45]

Robert E. Mortensen, president of the board of port commissioners, reacted angrily to Davis' decision that further employment plans would have to be approved prior to approval of the overrun. On February 7 he wrote Davis that "The project has been inordinately delayed and today we have progressed no further than the preliminary design stage. We have attempted to keep this project moving toward realization. However, it appears to us that EDA may not share our sense of urgency in causing the project to be implemented. I believe our impression is supported by EDA's delay in processing our additional assistance application."[46] Davis responded to Mortensen on February 11, saying that the port commissioner's letter was in no way responsive to the EDA position. The assistant secretary stated that he looked forward to meeting with port officials in the hope that some understanding could be reached.[47]

A meeting did take place, on February 14, between EDA officials, the Port of Oakland, World Airways, Mayor Reading, and Oakland's Congressmen Cohelan and Miller. According to Davis, "the Port said that they'd wait and deal with the Republicans. I said you don't know what the Republicans will do and maybe you'd better deal with me."[48] With a new EDA head soon to be named, the port reasoned that a less rigid attitude might come to the agency. Neither side was willing to change its posture. The next day Ross Davis sent the port commissioners a list of minimum requirements for an employment plan. It would have to provide for an employment officer,

45. EDA guidelines, January 31, 1969. Included in letter from Davis to Peter M. Tripp, president, Board of Port Commissioners, January 31, 1969.
46. Letter from Mortensen to Davis, February 7, 1969.
47. Letter from Davis to Mortensen, February 11, 1969.
48. Davis interview.

intensive recruiting of minorities, and the making of changes in civil service requirements to facilitate minority hiring.[49]

Meanwhile, the estimated cost of the hangar continued to rise. On February 18 Mortensen notified Davis that new projections set the eventual cost at $16,234,000, a rise of over $1 million since early 1968. Further EDA assistance would be necessary, said Mortensen.[50] The next day Mortensen sent Davis the port's "Tentative Statement of Employment Policy," which pledged that the port would "assist the City in establishing an Equal Employment Opportunity Program and a position of Equal Employment Opportunity Officer for the City including the Port of Oakland."[51] (The EDA had asked the port to create such a position for the port itself.) The plan also pledged that the port would work with community groups to recruit and hire more minorities.

World Airways was somewhat less cordial in its response to the EDA's demand. World's attorney, Jerome C. Byrne, wrote to Davis that the employment plan agreement would have to be replaced. Byrne explained:

This Agreement provides for an arbitration provision. My research indicates that agencies of the United States Government are not permitted to agree to arbitration of disputes without specific statutory authorization. I would be happy to provide you with my research in this area if you so desire. At any rate I assume that you will agree that EDA and World should not enter into any agreement that is not in accord with federal law.[52]

Because of these legal doubts (which EDA lawyers have challenged) and because World's MDTA training program had never materialized, Byrne proposed that an "amended" employment plan and agreement be adopted. The attorney enclosed in his letter the draft of a new employment plan which was rather vague in its promises and projections for hiring minority unemployed:

To the extent that the graduates of the East Bay Skills Center and other such training programs meet World's qualifications for employment and to the extent that World has openings for employees for entry level jobs, World will give precedence to the hiring of such graduates. . . . World and EDA

49. Letter from Davis to Board of Port Commissioners, February 15, 1969.
50. Letter from Mortensen to Davis, February 18, 1969.
51. "Tentative Statement of Employment Policy: Port of Oakland," February 1969. Enclosed in letter from Mortensen to Davis, February 19, 1969.
52. Letter from Byrne to Davis, February 20, 1969.

recognize the extreme complexity of predicting business expansion and recognize the speculative nature of training programs of organizations such as the East Bay Skills Center as to their ability to train the unemployed and the under-employed for entry level jobs in the airline industry. Recognizing these problems, World will, however, exert its best efforts to obtain qualified personnel from the sources heretofore mentioned, but cannot hold out any promises that any particular number of personnel will be hired from such sources.[53]

It was clear that the EDA and World were moving even farther apart.

On February 26, 1969, Ross Davis announced his long-awaited decision: the request for the overrun would not be approved. In a letter to Robert Mortensen of the Port Commission, Davis declared:

*As EDA has repeatedly stressed, the agency is not in the business of building aircraft hangars or other facilities for port authorities or business firms, particularly firms that have financial resources to build such facilities without government assistance.* EDA *is* in the business of creating jobs for the unemployed, the underemployed and the poor. In Oakland, California, this means jobs primarily for Negroes and Mexican-Americans.[54]

Davis criticized the performance of World Airways and the port in the area of jobs. There were, for instance, no Negroes or Mexican-Americans holding professional jobs within the Port of Oakland in 1968, according to an Oakland civil service report. The assistant secretary believed that attempts by the port and World to frame employment plans were unsatisfactory. The port had failed to provide for an equal opportunity officer in its own staff, and it had not committed itself to seeking changes in (and exemptions from) civil service requirements. Furthermore, the plan itself was "tentative"; it had never been approved by the port commissioners. World's new plan, in Davis' view, was "less satisfactory than the original Employment Plan Agreement of December 1966." The proposed revisions, he said, had failed "to enumerate the specific actions which World plans to undertake to hire the hard core unemployed Negroes, Mexican-Americans, or other minority groups in the Oakland community."[55]

On the same day, Davis wrote to World Airways President Ed-

53. Revised employment plan of World Airways, February 20, 1969.

54. Letter from Davis to Mortensen, February 26, 1969. Emphasis in original.

55. *Ibid.,* p. 6.

ward J. Daly to inform him of the decision. The assistant secretary asserted that "Despite EDA's extraordinary efforts to assist both the Port of Oakland and World Airways to come forward with Employment Plans responsive to the needs of Oakland's unemployed and underemployed residents, both the Port and World have failed to meet the minimum assurances that EDA sought."[56]

During the next month—Davis' last as head of EDA—some progress was made in creating an employment program at the port. On March 24 the port commissioners took the word "tentative" out of their employment policy. They agreed, furthermore, to give the Oakland city government $5,000 toward the $19,000 annual salary of a newly hired manpower consultant who was to "manage minority and disadvantaged employment programs for the city and the port."[57] Still, the EDA program was basically in a stalemate as the Nixon administration prepared to appoint a new head for the agency. Robert A. Podesta, an investment banker from Chicago, was named to replace Ross Davis as assistant secretary for EDA. Oakland's EDA recipients waited anxiously to see what the attitude of the new administration would be.

## A CHANGE OF ADMINISTRATION, 1969–70

Soon after taking office as assistant secretary, Podesta put his chief aide, Richard L. Sinnott, in charge of the Oakland program. Sinnott remembers that, "At that time, we had $30 million of commitments and $7 million of expenditures. We just put a freeze on Oakland projects, and treated each project—the hangar, the 7th Street terminal, the hotel—as a new application. The change in scope in all three gave us legal grounds to do so."[58] Podesta, Sinnott, and their staff decided to examine carefully the whole Oakland commitment. They "visited Oakland on a number of occasions—with the mayor, community leaders, black people, and the port."[59] To all these groups, the EDA officials gave the message that the agency would continue to insist on job creation for the unemployed as a necessary condition for the receipt of funds.

56. Letter from Davis to Daly, February 26, 1969.
57. "Port Takes Plunge on Hiring Policy," *Oakland Tribune,* March 25, 1969, p. 15.
58. Interview with Richard L. Sinnott, August 5, 1970.
59. *Ibid.*

During most of 1969 the terminal and hangar projects were held in abeyance while the EDA studied the problems surrounding those projects and possible ways of solving them. (The option of discontinuing the projects entirely continued to have supporters in the agency also.) Decisions had to be made on the following: Should the EDA approve the Port's plan for a revolving restaurant at the terminal? Should the EDA agree to increased funding for the hangar, in return for a binding employment agreement with World Airways? Or should the EDA refuse the overrun in any case?) What time limits should be placed on compliance with EDA conditions?

IMPLEMENTATION: MARINE TERMINAL

The Port of Oakland approved a new affirmative action policy in September 1969 that committed the port to hire an equal employment officer. That official would seek unemployed and underemployed candidates for port employment, propose training programs, assist the port in "seeking realistic employment standards," and direct counseling programs.[60] In early 1970 Joseph Barnett, a black employment specialist, was named to fill the new post. While the EDA considered the port's revolving restaurant plan, some progress was being made in 1969 on other parts of the terminal project. In April the navy withdrew its objections to the proposed construction when the port agreed to eliminate an offending crane.[61]

In June the Umpqua Company of Oregon was awarded a contract for filling and dredging at the terminal project. (The contract-awarding process was not without its problems. Twice before, bids had been thrown out by port attorneys. In the first instance, there was a problem with a minor amendment to the bid document. In the second instance, the low bid by Umpqua had been disallowed when it was discovered that the affidavit of noncollusion had not been dated properly. After some extended legal jockeying, Umpqua's bid was finally approved.) The filling and dredging began in mid-July, over three years after the announcement of the project.

As the year progressed, the new leaders of the EDA began to have serious doubts about the wisdom of approving the port's long-stand-

60. Port of Oakland statement of employment policy, September 8, 1969.
61. See letter from Admiral Janney to Frank Cirillo of the EDA, April 7, 1969.

ing request for a revolving restaurant. It would be a fancy project, they observed, which might make EDA look extravagant. The jobs produced would be low paying. Finally, the proposed lessee had had a disappointing record of minority hiring. But the EDA, under Ross Davis, had already decided to approve the revolving restaurant. If the new EDA leadership wanted to change the agency's policy, how could they justify such a decision? Fortunately for those in the EDA who opposed the revolving restaurant, an answer to the dilemma was at hand. As one federal official described it: "This is how we got out of Phase 3. We had actually approved final plans and specs including it. But we knew that there would be an overrun, a big one, for Phase 2 [construction of the terminal itself]. If the overrun was big enough, the Port would have to request money from Phase 3. And that's what happened. The restaurant was dropped as a *quid pro quo*."

On December 11 Assistant Secretary Podesta wrote to the port, announcing the EDA's decision not to participate in funding the revolving restaurant. The next day, the port's executive director, Ben Nutter, wrote to Podesta to acknowledge the decision. Nutter also had a request to make:

The construction bids for Phase II of the Seventh Street Main Terminal project have exceeded the EDA approved budgeted amount for this phase of the construction project. In response to your decision, we request that the $600,000.00 plus the 5% construction contingency of $30,000 budgeted for Phase III restaurant and public facilities construction be made available for Phase II construction and thereby serve to reduce our overage for this phase of the project.[62]

The EDA acceded to the request. By shifting funds from the revolving restaurant to cover an overrun on basic terminal construction, the federal agency was able to free itself from participation in a potentially embarrassing venture. The revolving restaurant might still be built, but the EDA would not be responsible for it.

In late December two construction contracts for the terminal project were awarded by the port. Ben C. Gerwick Company won a contract for $2,152,543 for construction of wharves, and Rothschild and Raffin, Inc. signed a $4,776,000 contract for constructing roads, a cargo transit shed, and utilities.[63]

62. Letter from Nutter to Podesta, December 12, 1969.
63. "$6.9 Million in Port Jobs OK'd," *Oakland Tribune,* December 25, 1969, p. 6.

During the next year the long-awaited construction of the 7th Street terminal actually began to take place. By December 1, 1970, the EDA's Office of Public Works reported that the terminal was "78 percent complete." Two transit sheds, the paving of 7th Street and the container area, and the installation of some sewers were yet to be completed.[64] But after four and a half years of waiting, a marine terminal *was* being built.

IMPLEMENTATION: WORLD AIRWAYS HANGAR

If the marine terminal project was beginning to show some signs of progress, such was not the case with the EDA's most difficult project, the airline hangar. On August 29, 1969, the port requested that the EDA deviate from its established policy of two-stage (design-construction) competitive bidding and allow the port to negotiate a contract with one firm for both design and construction. The EDA's Office of Public Works took a dim view of such a procedure, feeling that there would be no "checks and balances" between designer and builder if one firm did all the work. Besides, the EDA wanted to review the final plans before construction bids were let.[65] The Office of Public Works was frank to note that some of its misgivings "result from disappointment with regard to the Port and the manner in which it has dragged its feet in the past three years."[66] Once again, memos were written that explored the justification for terminating the project altogether.

By early 1970 the EDA leadership had decided not to cut off the project at that point, but to attach additional stringent conditions to continuation of support for the hangar. On February 2, 1970, Deputy Assistant Secretary Sinnott wrote to Ben Nutter to inform him that the port's request for design-and-construction contracting had been denied: "The EDA program is one which should respond with some dispatch and with some meaning to the target population. This project has not met that test. At this stage, therefore, we are not prepared to agree to a construction procedure which on the surface suggests short cuts and time saving, but which adds to the uncertainty of the kind of facility that will eventually be constructed."[67]

64. Information received from the EDA Office of Public Works. See Table 6.
65. Memo from George Karras to Richard Sinnott, January 13, 1970.
66. *Ibid.*
67. Letter from Sinnott to Nutter, February 12, 1970.

Although Sinnott declared that the EDA intended to "fulfill its commitment," he specified that fulfillment would only take place under certain conditions: the cost of construction had to be under $9,550,000; original job expectations had to be met; final plans and specifications—including the lower cost—had to be completed by December 31, 1970. Sinnott pointed out that "close to four years have transpired since this grant and loan offer was accepted and we cannot permit this offer to remain open indefinitely." This was the EDA's hardest line to date.

Responding to the EDA's demand that the cost of the hangar be drastically cut, the port switched the A/E assignment from Charles Luckman to the firm of Strobel and Rongved of New York. The new firm promised to design "a Ford, not a Cadillac,"[68] and proposed a reduction in the hangar's building size of 16 percent. Preliminary plans and specifications submitted to the EDA in June 1970 estimated the cost at $9.2 million, well within EDA guidelines. The EDA approved preliminary plans and specifications on June 30. The Port Commission approved the revised project in early July, although Commissioner Robert Mortensen voted against the proposal on the grounds that there was no guarantee that the EDA would ever agree to finance the hangar. "I can't act affirmatively on hearsay," Mortensen declared. "After three years there is still no EDA approval and no employment agreement from World."[69] EDA officials, after a brief period of enthusiasm about the new low cost estimates, began to doubt in the late summer whether they were realistic.

World Airways' employment intentions continued to provide still another focus of controversy. John E. Corrigan, director of the EDA Office of Equal Opportunity, went to Oakland to try to work out an acceptable affirmative action employment plan with World. The airline company submitted a long document on May 15, but Corrigan's staff found a number of weaknesses in it: the geographical area for hiring was considered to be the East Bay area, not Oakland; there were no concrete programs spelled out for training minorities to fill professional jobs; there was inadequate specification of the sources of minority recruitment.[70]

68. "Jumbo Jet Hangar Proposal Approved," *Oakland Tribune,* July 3, 1970, p. 18.

69. *Ibid.*

70. Staff criticisms enclosed in letter from John E. Corrigan to General Howell M. Estes, Jr., vice-president of World Airways, July 2, 1970.

Not only was World's affirmative action program considered to be inadequate in its plans for minority hiring; federal officials were also critical of its treatment of women. Quentin S. Taylor, director of civil rights for the Federal Aviation Agency, wrote Corrigan on June 19: "I am greatly concerned about the statement on page 111, under 'Child Care Assistance,' which says that 'female employees are not among those training positions.' This appears to be a violation of the new OFCC [Office of Federal Contract Compliance] sex guidelines. . . . It does not appear that sex would be a bona fide occupational qualification for trainee positions in the aircraft trades."[71] The gulf between World Airways and the EDA was not getting much narrower—four years after the hangar project (the "keystone" of the EDA program) had been announced.

While relations between the EDA and World Airways remained cool during 1970, those between World and the port became frigid. On November 18 the *Oakland Tribune* announced in a headline: "PORT TO CANCEL WORLD AIR AGREEMENT IN DISPUTE." The article said that "Oakland port commissioners will cancel the license agreements of World Airways for hangar and office space in an attempt to get the airline into negotiations on increased rental fees. . . . That action by the board yesterday followed a report by port staff members who said they did not receive any response from World regarding a month-old notification of proposed increases." One of the World projects affected, said the *Tribune*, would be the EDA-financed hangar, which had been "three years in discussion and design."[72] Finally, in June of 1971, although disagreements between the port and World had not been fully resolved, the port awarded construction contracts for the hangar.

SOME LOCAL INITIATIVES

When Hugh Taylor became head of the EDA Oakland office in December 1968, he felt that "the most important thing was to get promised performance before we get any new promises."[73] When contracts for construction of the marine terminal were about to be let in late 1969, Taylor tried to ensure that construction jobs would go to minority workers. Office of Federal Contract Compliance (OFCC)

71. Letter from Quentin S. Taylor to John E. Corrigan, June 19, 1970.
72. *Oakland Tribune,* November 18, 1970.
73. Interview with Hugh Taylor, November 30, 1970.

guidelines required pre-bid affirmative action plans to be approved, and Taylor and his assistant, James Clark, decided to use that provision to secure minority hiring. "That guideline is only a piece of paper; it depends on what you do to enforce it," Taylor remarked.[74]

In late 1969 Oakland EDA officials began to work with the port in organizing the bidding process. At a pre-bidding conference on November 14, Taylor and Corrigan of the EDA—together with an enforcement officer from OFCC—took a hard line with potential contractors. The federal officials explained that all bids had to be accompanied by affirmative action plans. On November 25 the bids were opened, and on December 2 the bidders were invited in again for a preaward conference. At that meeting EDA representatives told the bidders that the federal agency was interested in minority contracting—joint ventures with minority subcontractors and subcontracting with minority enterprises. All general contractors and subcontractors would have to have affirmative action programs or payments would be suspended by the EDA.

When the bids and affirmative action plans were examined, the EDA decided that the low bidder for the roads and sheds part of the project—Rothschild and Raffin, Inc.—did not have a strong or specific enough affirmative action proposal. EDA Oakland officials would not approve the awarding of a contract to Rothschild and Raffin until changes were made in the plan.

Under EDA proddings, Rothschild and Raffin produced an affirmative action plan that was more specific than those signed by previous EDA beneficiaries. The contracting firm named the minority-owned subcontractors with whom it would work, and it named specific percentages of minority workers who would be employed. In a letter to the port, Rothschild and Raffin stated,

In the minor excavation for the underpass we propose to use one half minority men. In order to accomplish this, we will need the complete cooperation of the Federal Agencies. For trucking we propose to use Soul Trucking, the bulkheading will be done by predominately minority carpenters and laborers from Oakland. The concrete underpass will also be framed and poured by minority carpenters and laborers from Oakland. There is a small building on which we have asked minority subcontractors—Oliver Shavies and Archie Tademy—to submit a proposal. We have also asked them to submit a proposal for the foundation of the warehouse. We are attaching copies of

74. *Ibid.*

those letters. . . . We will have an Oakland minority worker in the job office, to take care of the time keeping and job paper work. We are enclosing copy of our usual reporting form of breakdown of ethnic groups on the project. We also enclose manpower projection of the various items of work.[75]

With reference to construction of transit sheds, architectural building, and wall panels, Rothschild and Raffin announced its intention to have the work done "using a black crew from the Oakland area."

Potential subcontractors for the project were also required to list the number and race of people they would employ. For example, E. H. Morrill Company pledged that

The employee composition for E. H. Morrill Co. on the Port of Oakland job will be as follows:
Four plumbers:
  1 foreman
  1 negro journeyman
  1 negro apprentice
  1 non-minority journeyman
Three laborers:
  3 minority laborers
The cooperation of Plumbers' Local 444 has been assured by Mr. Hess.[76]

EDA Oakland officials were now requiring more of contractors than a simple pledge to "try their best" on hiring minorities; potential recipients of EDA funding now had to promise that they would employ certain numbers of minority workers.

Yet, as EDA participants constantly pointed out, enforcement of plans is difficult. One agency official estimated that about 300 construction jobs had been created at the terminal project by November 1970, about 60 percent of which were held by minority workers. But he added a cautionary note: "That's about 60% on peak days, with a lower percentage on non-peak days. And out of those 300 jobs, only about 70 are craftsmen's jobs. That is the focus of the struggle—for jobs on the permanent staff. They can hire blacks for short time periods and move them around from project to project, but permanent jobs are what we want to get. Future agreements should try to secure permanent jobs on a construction company's staff."

Although the EDA had declared that payments would be sus-

75. Letter from R. B. Rothschild to the Port of Oakland, December 16, 1969.
76. Letter from David D. Nolan, attorney for E. H. Morrill Co., to Rothschild and Raffin, December 15, 1969.

pended for noncompliance with the affirmative action plans, Washington EDA officials have not been as ready as their Oakland counterparts to use these sanctions. Thus, although Oakland EDA officials were successful in negotiating far more specific affirmative action agreements for minority hiring, implementation and enforcement of those plans still posed problems in 1972.

In his time as EDA Oakland representative, Taylor has been active in supporting technical assistance projects that go directly to minority groups. In 1969 the EDA awarded a technical assistance grant of $94,000 to a Mexican-American group for the planning of a Spanish-speaking community center. Taylor and Clark of the EDA office were also instrumental in stimulating a joint HUD-EDA-Department of Labor project (the "Prep" program), which funds a minority contractor's association (General and Specialty Contractors Association) to refurbish homes in the West Oakland ghetto and to train minority youth. In a separate project, the EDA provided General and Specialty Contractors with a fifteen-month $75,000 grant to organize and provide technical assistance to minority contractors.[77]

Although some concrete gains were made after five years of EDA activity in Oakland, progress was slow. An agency official echoed a continual EDA concern when he discussed the need for supportive action in the local community: "We need enforcement activities; we need people to make demands for employment opportunities. And these demands ought to come from the local community." In the early days of the EDA Oakland program, federal officials had assumed that community groups would put pressure on aid recipients to force them to hire minorities. But the "non-group, non-political" nature of Oakland's social environment has meant that the sources for such pressure have been largely nonexistent. In an effort to alter this situation, local EDA officials have been supportive of the efforts of an ad hoc committee for minority employment in the downtown civic center project. The EDA hopes eventually to complete a loan agreement with a hotel company that will move into the project.

PROGRESS REPORT: DECEMBER 1970

On December 1, 1970, the EDA Office of Public Works released a report on the progress of its projects in Oakland. Table 4 shows the

77. Taylor interview.

TABLE 4: *Status of EDA Public Works Projects Oakland, California* (December 1, 1970)

| EDA Project Number | Description | EDA Funds | | | | Jobs | | Current Status |
|---|---|---|---|---|---|---|---|---|
| | | Approved | | Disbursed | | Anticipated | Actual | |
| | | Grant | Loan | Grant | Loan | | | |
| 07-1-00046 | 7th St. marine terminal | $6,075,000 | $4,050,000 | $4,284,200 | $4,050,000 | 175 | 1,000 | 78% complete; two transit sheds, paving of 7th Street and container area, and some sewers yet to be completed |
| 07-1-00049 | industrial park | 1,260,000 | 840,000 | 962,521 | 700,000 | 420 | 30 | 100% complete |
| 07-1-00050 | aircraft maint. hangar | 6,390,000 | 4,260,000 | 0 | 675,000 | 1,276 | N/A | Preliminary plans complete and under review by EDA consultant |
| 07-1-00051 | small aircraft hangar | 76,000 | 76,000 | 74,497 | 76,000 | 12 | 0 | 100% complete |
| 07-1-00052 | air cargo terminal | 244,000 | 184,000 | 219,000 | 184,000 | 20 | 250 (Relocated) | Work completed; Port of Oakland and contractor have pending lawsuit for alleged delays by contractor |
| 07-1-00160 | access road | 414,000 | 0 | 414,000 | 0 | 0 | N/A | 100% complete |
| 07-1-00294 | aircraft control tower | 133,800 | 89,000 | 0 | 10,000 | indirect creation of jobs | N/A | Design complete; further progress dependent on construction of 07-1-00050 |
| 07-1-00541 | West Oakland Health Center | 765,000 | 765,000 | 742,451 | 737,208 | 130 | 160 | 100% complete except for transfer of 2 parcels of land; EDA funds for acquisition of these parcels are being held by EDA until transfer is effected |

Source: Economic Development Administration, Office of Public Works.

status in terms of money expended, construction completed, and jobs produced of projects at that time. A number of cautionary words about this table are in order. The 1,000 actual jobs listed for the marine terminal are jobs involved in the "operation of the entire terminal,"[78] not just the one-third of the terminal that is EDA financed. (These jobs are actually in the *other* two-thirds of the terminal, in the non-EDA part that has been completed.) Out of the 1,000 jobs, an agency representative estimated that 350 have gone to minorities. The EDA feels justified in counting these jobs as EDA-induced, because if the EDA had not come in, the port would not have built the 7th Street terminal.

The 30 jobs at the industrial park are all for American Toy Company, and the 250 jobs for the air cargo terminal are for Universal Airlines. This airline company relocated at the air cargo terminal and an EDA official noted that "most of these jobs are not new." There were no available records on the number of these jobs held by unemployed minorities. The access road was felt by an EDA man to be the kind of project "that would not generate jobs in and of itself. But it may generate indirect jobs." These jobs would be very difficult to measure.

The chart does show some gains in the 1968–1970 period: construction on the marine terminal was under way and was 78 percent complete; the West Oakland Health Center had been completed and 160 jobs had been created, with about 150 going to minorities. An EDA representative estimates that 65 of these workers came from the ranks of the hard-core unemployed. (Implementation of the West Oakland Health Center is discussed in chapter 4.)

Thus, EDA officials estimated that the following numbers of jobs were created for minorities: 350 at the marine terminal and 150 at the West Oakland Health Center, for a total of 500. (We have been unable to obtain figures on the number of jobs for minorities created at American Toy Company and Universal Airlines.) In addition, construction of the marine terminal provided approximately 180 construction jobs for minorities.

Five years after the hope-filled genesis of the EDA Oakland program in late 1965, there were still major obstacles to fulfillment of the agency's goal of providing jobs for the hard-core unemployed of the inner city. World Airways and the EDA had still not agreed on a

78. Information received from Office of Public Works, December 6, 1970.

final plan for construction of the hangar, which was supposed to create 1,200 jobs and to be the most important segment of the program. Furthermore, the training programs that were to prepare the hard-core unemployed for employment had become snarled in the bureaucratic jungle of intergovernmental and interagency relations. Finally, in the projects that had been completed (like the industrial park) or were under construction (like the marine terminal), the EDA was not finding it at all easy to enforce employment demands. (By May 1971, construction of the terminal had been completed, and in June contracts were finally let for constructing the hangar. But the question of jobs lay ahead.)

It might be argued that, even though the EDA experienced difficulties in the implementation of its public works program, the agency did provide some unanticipated long-term benefits to poor people in Oakland. For example, EDA officials in the city aided in the development of the Opportunities Industrialization Center and the mayor's Manpower Commission. Also, agency representatives used technical assistance money to aid minority contractors. But we have found it difficult to identify specific unanticipated increases in minority employment that can be ascribed to the EDA. Besides, the public works effort was always felt to be the heart of the agency's Oakland program.

In *Oakland's Not for Burning* Amory Bradford describes the reaction of the members of the Oakland EDA task force to the project announcements of April 29, 1966: "As we listened, all of us who had been working on this felt a sense of tremendous relief. We had done all that we had set out to do, and more, and we had done it on time."[79] The congressional appropriations, agency commitment of funds, approval of projects and acceptance of the employment plan idea had all gone quickly and according to plan. But the "technical details" of financing, construction, and relations with other governmental agencies—combined with continued disagreements between the EDA and its potential beneficiaries about employment policy—had provided continual problems for five long years. Chains of unanticipated decision points, requiring numerous clearances by different actors, had provided the occasions for frustrating delays. The hopeful "experimental program" of 1966 had become a painful example of the problems of implementation.

79. Bradford, p. 124.

# 4

## Two Smaller Programs:
## Business Loans and the Health Center

The public works effort was not the only EDA program attempted in Oakland. At his April 1966 news conference, Assistant Secretary Foley had announced that a program of loans to businesses would create 800 new jobs in the city. EDA leaders saw the business loans program as a way of involving private sector firms of various sizes in the effort to provide jobs for the unemployed. But contradictory and restrictive legislative criteria, administrative conflicts, and disappointing performances by local firms combined to erect insuperable hazards to implementation of this program in Oakland.

By the end of 1968 EDA officials were becoming increasingly frustrated and depressed by delays in their Oakland program. They began to wonder if a project would ever be completed. So they seized on an existing neighborhood initiative in order to help bring a health center to West Oakland. Although this center was not part of the 1966 EDA initiative, we include a brief account of it at the end of this chapter to provide a little illumination in an otherwise bleak scene. Later, when we want to contrast a program that has succeeded with others that did not, we will have something with which to work.

### BUSINESS LOANS: GOING FROM THE MERELY DIFFICULT
### TO THE REALLY IMPOSSIBLE

Policy implementation is made difficult when experience reveals that legislators want incompatible things. They want to help people in areas of low employment by attracting new industries or expanding old ones. But they do not want to subsidize competitors against their own people. When their constituents complain that government funds are being spent to support business competitors, the congressmen naturally write in provisions stating that aid to industry must not compete with existing firms. Since most conceivable enterprises compete in some way with others, the dilemma is passed on to the administrators who discover that they cannot apply the criteria with any consistency. This is one moral of the EDA business loans program.

Both the legislation and the information leaflets of the EDA claim that private enterprise is the key to remedying unemployment in depressed regions. A message from the assistant secretary of commerce on an information folder says, "The federal government, through EDA, can help with this task, but only private enterprise can get the unemployed off the relief roll and onto a payroll." In the United States Senate, following introduction of the public works and economic development bill, Senator Proxmire explained that he liked the bill because it stressed "private enterprise and private development," did not provide for a "gigantic federally controlled and directed public works program," and "basic investment decisions [would] be left up to the private sector of our economy."[1]

And yet the appropriations heavily favor public works expenditure over the business loans program.[2] Why? The idea behind funding public infrastructure is to make a depressed area more attractive to private industry. Public spending is seen as pump priming for the private economy in the area. During the introduction of the public works and economic development bill to the Senate, most of the supporting evidence emphasized that the new bill was to replace the Accelerated Public Works Act program which was expiring at the time. At this stage, public works financing was seen primarily as a means of creating jobs to ease unemployment until the anticipated effect of the tax cut became apparent. The emphasis on public works

1. U.S. Senate, Congressional Record, May 26, 1965, p. 11799.
2. The annual appropriations, from 1966 to 1970, provided $500 million in grants, $170 million in loans. While private business may only receive loans, public works projects may receive grants and loans.

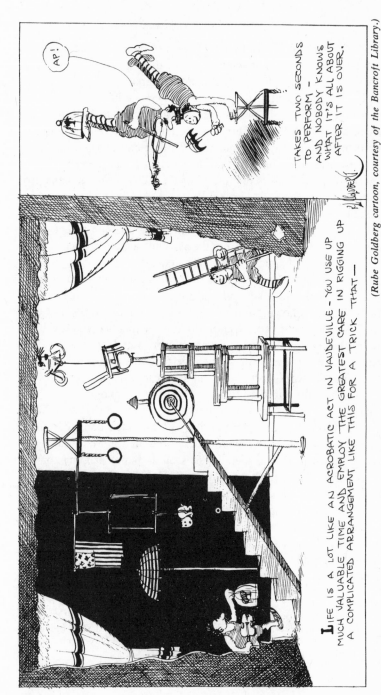

(*Rube Goldberg cartoon, courtesy of the Bancroft Library.*)

THAT'S AN AWFUL LOT OF WORK FOR NOTHING.

spending as a means of encouraging the development of private enterprise arose as the bill went through the legislative process.[3]

We shall see that those federal and local actors who had dealings with Oakland's business loan program had numerous reasons for becoming disillusioned with it. How did this program, which initially engendered so much support both in Congress and at the local level, eventually engender both bitterness and disillusionment? One answer would seem to lie in a dilemma central to such intervention programs.

The use of public money to stimulate private enterprise rather than to mount public works programs has considerable appeal for many congressmen and their constituents. But in practice such programs soon cause resentment among that same constituency because they inevitably subsidize, or in other ways assist, some firms while ignoring others. William C. Heyn, giving evidence before the Senate Public Works Committee, described the dilemma when he argued that "It is unfair to existing industry to use their tax money to subsidize new industry which will compete for their markets" and that, "since industrial development is a highly competitive activity, it is unfair and discriminatory for the Federal Government to take sides in behalf of some areas, thereby working against other areas to create competition for their products and jobs."[4]

From the time the Area Redevelopment Administration (ARA) began its business loans program, this problem was aggravated by the fact that the average unemployment level was quite high. It is difficult to redistribute jobs from the rich to the poor regions when even the richest regions are short of jobs themselves. Levitan points out that "it is difficult to defend government financing of new capacity when established firms operate below their optimum level because of inadequate demand,"[5] and Miernyk observes that, "When the level

3. U.S. Senate, Congressional Record, May 26, 1965, pp. 11787–11799.

4. U.S. House of Representatives, Public Works Committee Hearings, Public Works and Economic Development Act of 1965, 89th Congress, 1st Session, April 26–May 3, 1965, statement of William C. Heyn, assistant to the president, New Holland Machine Co., Division of Sperry-Rand, New Holland, Pennsylvania, on behalf of the National Association of Manufacturers, p. 156.

5. Sar Levitan, *Federal Aid to Depressed Areas* (Johns Hopkins University Press, 1964), p. 247.

of unemployment is rising, and when unemployment is widespread, little can be done to alleviate the chronic unemployment of the depressed areas."[6]

The severe criticism leveled at the ARA because of the charge of robbing Peter to pay Paul resulted in the introduction of constraining legislation into the Public Works and Economic Development Act of 1965. The chairman was fully aware of the touchiness of this issue when he emphasized, in his introductory statement before the Senate Public Works Committee, that the bill was not designed to "take from one area for the benefit of another," or to "shift job opportunities from our more prosperous communities to the less prosperous," or to "enhance the growth potential of one region to the detriment of another."[7] The legislation reflects this concern by placing restraints on the business loans program. "No financial assistance under this Act shall be extended to any project when the result would be to increase the production of goods, materials, or commodities, or the availability of services or facilities, when there is not sufficient demand for such goods, material, commodities, services, or facilities, to employ the efficient capacity of existing competitive commercial or industrial enterprises."[8]

This is not an easy requirement to administer. At a hearing before the Special Subcommittee on Economic Development Programs, Mr. Edmonson (chairman) asked Ross Davis (assistant secretary of commerce for economic development) how his staff was handling it.[9] Davis replied that the vagueness of, and difficulty of quantifying, such terms as "sufficient demand," "efficient capacity," and "existing competitive enterprises" was making "translation from concept to a specific practical situation quite difficult." He asked, for example, under what economic circumstances and over what period of time "sufficient demand" was to be interpreted.

6. William H. Miernyk, quoted from testimony before U.S. Senate Committee on Labor and Public Welfare, Subcommittee on Labor, Hearings on Area Redevelopment, 84th Congress, 2nd Session, p. 154.

7. U.S. Senate, Public Works Committee Hearings, Public Works and Economic Development Act of 1965, p. 2.

8. Public Works and Economic Development Act, 1965, Sec. 702.

9. U.S. House of Representatives, Hearings Before the Special Subcommittee on Economic Development Programs, 90th Congress, 1st Session, April 11, 1967, pp. 15–17.

To legislators the issue was simple. As Congressman Cleveland explained, "I wonder if it would not be helpful to you if we worked that from the other end? Put yourself in the place of a Congressman. The telephone rings. It is a constituent. The constituent wants to know from his Congressman why the Government is building a motel right next to his motel when he only has half of his available motel facilities used. This constituent is paying taxes."[10]

The EDA administrator is being asked to evaluate businesses to ensure that they are not competing with other firms, are not taking jobs from other areas, and are only producing new jobs in the economy and that the capacity of all other producers in that field is fully taxed, all within a frame of reference undetermined in both space and time. The administrator would also be aware that during the ARA operation the funding of businesses that offended in any of these regards had resulted in much criticism being directed at the agency and its staff.[11] Under these conditions, it is not so much surprising that loans took so long to process (a common complaint of local businessmen) as it is remarkable that any were processed at all.

PROJECT DECISIONS

The affection of Congress for employment, as we have seen, was real but not total. New jobs for the poor were good so long as they did not displace other people. The men who administered these provisions, however, did not share all the qualms and pressures felt by the legislators. Congress may have written the language, but the administrators were doing the translating.

Not surprisingly, EDA administrators took a dim view of the statutory criteria for loans. Figure 1 shows the incredibly complex and contradictory decision path which, according to the legislation, the EDA would have to follow. Faced with this administrator's nightmare, the business loans division of the EDA devised some shortcuts. A former loan official of the agency declared, "We didn't really fol-

10. *Ibid.*, p. 17. Sundquist notes that "ARA-financed motels in depressed areas were made to appear as threats to every existing motel for miles around," p. 106, in *Politics and Policy: The Eisenhower, Kennedy, and Johnson Years* (Washington, D.C.: Brookings Institution, 1968).
11. Levitan, pp. 124–130.

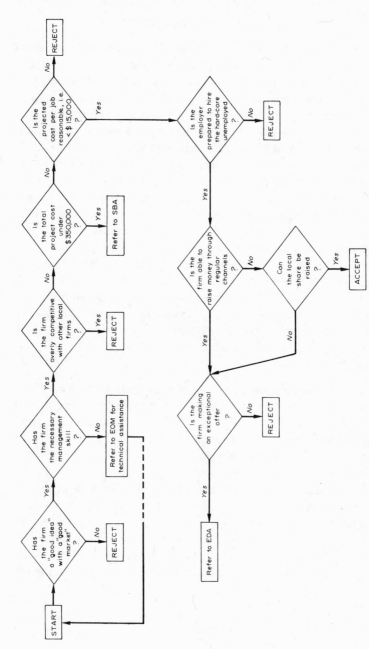

FIGURE 1. The business loans decision tree, according to legislation

low the statutory criteria—all that stuff about not being competitive and not being able to get money from any other source. That was put in by Congressmen who wanted to ruin the program. What we did pay attention to was whether the firm was a dying industry or had excess capacity. In these cases, we wouldn't give loans."

For the Oakland experiment, EDA loan procedures were altered significantly. Normally, EDA field coordinators would develop a project. If an application was filed, it was then sent to the EDA in Washington. A project review committee there met with its counterpart from the Small Business Administration's Washington office. That committee reviewed the application. If the committee's decision was favorable, the SBA was given a set of instructions and asked to conduct a credit investigation. (For the most part, SBA staff members served as the EDA loan division's field personnel. This "delegate agency" device was an economy measure that had been advocated by the Budget Bureau.) After the credit investigation, the SBA wrote a report and sent it to the EDA field office. The EDA reviewed the credit information and made a judgment on job-producing capacity. Finally, the application would come back to the loan director's office for approval or disapproval. A former loan official observed that "the whole thing took about six months. It's true that the target was ninety days. But very few took less than ninety days—the average was about six months."

For Oakland, the process was different:

We put an EDA loan specialist—Daschbach—directly into Oakland. We coordinated efforts with SBA in San Francisco. Our specialist developed a project and reported back to EDA on the project being developed. We'd then discuss the application with Daschbach, a deputy here in the office, and the head of business loans for the western U.S. For Oakland, we ignored the EDA area office and the SBA-EDA Project Review Committee. SBA completed the field investigation and the report was sent directly to EDA.

There were two steps for Oakland: (1) Daschbach and SBA would submit a field report; (2) Washington EDA would examine it. The process of decision was shortened (fewer people were involved) and concentrated (less geographic distance per encounter). Daschbach viewed his own role as that of a promoter, defending projects against the attacks of lawyers, financial engineers, and other agency officials.

Thus we see that the bureaucracy assigned an expediter to circumvent its own restrictions.

For Daschbach, the major criterion for approving applications was the relation of jobs to dollars. The ratio had to be less than $15,-000 per job. The EDA loan office sets up cost/job guidelines to evaluate job-producing potential and to ensure that EDA participation in a project will be kept within bounds; applicants are encouraged to seek money from other sources as well.

The problem was that there were not very many good applicants, that is, businesses that the EDA felt would provide new jobs for inner-city unemployed. Staff members interviewed remembered that only "about a dozen" good applications ever came in. Faced with a paucity of good applications, the EDA in its decisions "went for diversity," according to a former agency official. "We decided to make a loan to one Negro entrepreneur, one project that would provide jobs for the low end of the labor scale, and one business that would provide reasonably skilled jobs." This official noted that "criteria were not something we started with and judged things by. We formulated the criteria *after* we saw what Daschbach brought in. We figured out some things that might be done and decided to get one example of each." (There was no funding constraint; the EDA was far below its permissible loan total of $10 million for Oakland.)

The EDA decided to approve loans for Bennie's Candies (the black entrepreneur); Rainbow Car Wash (for the lower end of the economic scale); and Colombo Bakery ("reasonably skilled jobs"). Also approved was a loan to Sierra Cotton Mills; a loan to Berkeley Instruments (electronic telemetry manufacturing) had been approved in January. The awarding of all these loans could not, of course, be made officially until the approval of employment plans by the review board was secured; this was not done until the fall.

The 5 percent local share provided some difficulty in the administration of the loan program; the EDA legislation required that the local community make a cash contribution as a means of promoting community involvement and participation in the program. The ARA had had a similar requirement, and in 1965 Mayor Houlihan had asked that the business community become involved in the federal economic development program. He established the Oakland Economic Development Foundation (OEDF), which was a group of businessmen who were to provide the local share required for federal loans.

Numerous members of the 1966 EDA staff in Oakland criticized the OEDF as being an obstacle to the loan program ("Those people didn't even believe in federal programs"). When the foundation was asked to give its approval to the first two business loan applicants (Colombo Bakery and Sierra Cotton Mills), the foundation turned down both applications, arguing that Colombo did not need low cost federal loans for its expansion and that Sierra was a bad risk. Bradford did not accept this explanation and claimed that the foundation "had little feel for the problems of expanding small businesses and new ventures" and that "they seemed to feel that anyone who applied for a government loan because he could not get financing through commercial channels was a bad risk."[12]

In order to avoid further such delay, neither the Bennie's Candies nor the Rainbow Car Wash proposals were presented to the foundation for approval. The OEDF was one example of "citizen participation" that didn't work.[13]

THE OUTCOME OF BUSINESS LOANS

Table 5 presents the disappointing results of the EDA business loans projects, as of October 1968.

*Colombo Baking Company* appears to have used the loan "to finance expansion and automation rather than employment positions."[14] The EDA internal report states that "it is apparent that Colombo did not need a loan from EDA. Clearly Colombo was in a financial position to seek and get commercial money or possibly finance the proposed expansion itself."[15] The report outlines Colombo's minimal progress in the field of job creation:

Colombo had 109 employees when they applied for an EDA loan to finance bulk flour storage facilities. Colombo now employs 117. During that period one employee left (a Negro who became a minority entrepreneur—without government assistance). Of the new hires, three have been Negroes. One

12. Amory Bradford, *Oakland's Not for Burning* (New York: McKay, 1968), p. 62.
13. Pp. 73–76 of this chapter were adapted from Owen McShane, "Toward a Transitional Economics" (unpublished paper, April 1970).
14. *Ibid.*, p. 53.
15. EDA internal report, p. 44.

TABLE 5: EDA Business Loans in Oakland Produce Few Jobs at High Cost: EDA Expenditures and Resulting Jobs

| Name and Type of Firm | Total Project Cost ($) | EDA Loan ($) | Projected Jobs | Projected Total Cost/Job($) | Projected EDA Cost/Job($) | Actual Jobs | Actual Total Cost/Job($) | Actual EDA Cost/Job($) |
|---|---|---|---|---|---|---|---|---|
| Colombo Baking Co. (rejected by OEDF) | 650,000 | 423,000 | 158 | 4,114 | 2,677 | 8 | 81,250 | 52,875 |
| Bennie's Candies | 99,000 | 73,000 | 25 | 3,960 | 2,920 | 10 | 9,900 | 7,300 |
| Rainbow Car Wash | 207,000 | 135,000 | 35 | 5,914 | 3,857 | 25 | 8,280 | 5,400 |
| Sierra Cotton Mills (rejected by OEDF) | — | 376,000 | 66 | — | 5,697 | BANKRUPT | | |
| Berkeley Instruments (electronic telemetry manufacturing) | 120,000 | 78,000 | 25 | 4,500 | 3,120 | BANKRUPT | | |
| National Plug (scrap paper reprocessing) | 45,000 (undisbursed) | | 25 | — | 1,800 | WITHDREW | | |
| Value Engineering (pipe fabrication) | 450,000 | 280,000 (undisbursed) | 26 | 17,308 | 10,769 | WITHDREW | | |
| Hyatt Hotel Corporation | 13,000,000 | '4,000,000 (not yet disbursed) | 763 | 17,038 | 5,242 | BEING PROCESSED | | |

Source: Owen McShane, "Toward A Transitional Economics," pp. 55, 58. Figures based on 1968 EDA internal report.

of the four other Negro employes was upgraded through use of on-the-job training assistance (Federal money). This young lady was moved from a job in the bakery to the outer office as receptionist.[16]

*Bennie's Candies* is owned by Bennie Smith, a black entrepreneur who wanted to expand from an over-the-counter family business into a larger commercial enterprise. His EDA loan was for plant and equipment, but the equipment expenditure—for a candy machine— was a disaster. The 1968 EDA report is critical of the SBA's joint role in the process:

The SBA's engineering review failed to adequately evaluate the capacity of a jam-making machine to dispense molten peanut praline batter. SBA's failure to include a clause in the purchase contract with Food Machinery Corporation which would have required performance of the equipment, and SBA's disbursement of money for final payment on the equipment before evaluating its ability to meet its requirements have brought Bennie near the point of failure.[17]

In simpler terms, the brand new candy machine failed to work.

The EDA business loans office tried to get their agency to provide Bennie with technical assistance (in the form of management men) to help him with financial affairs. But the agency's technical assistance officials argued that this would be a subterfuge for giving him working capital, which the agency was not supposed to do. If a man needed all that assistance, they reasoned, then he was obviously not a good businessman.Bennie had to get working capital from the SBA, which let the money out "in drips and drabs," as Bennie said. Instead of giving him the entire working capital loan of $25,000 to put in the bank, the SBA would provide no more than $1,000 at a time.[18] Under these conditions "black capitalism" was a hazardous enterprise. A potentially antagonistic administrative relationship had thus been built into loan program implementation. The EDA was interested in stimulating growth and creating jobs, while SBA viewed projects with a cautious banker's eye. Yet according to a Budget Bureau directive, EDA programs had to rely on SBA staff for working capital assistance.

*Rainbow Car Wash* produced twenty-five jobs at the bottom end

16. *Ibid.*
17. *Ibid.,* pp. 45–46.
18. Owen McShane interview with Bennie Smith, April 30, 1970.

of the economic ladder. Although these jobs were criticized as "dead end," they represented a reasonably successful investment for the EDA: the federal agency's cost per job was only $5,400.

*Sierra Cotton Mills* in 1968 was "in the position of imminent fore-closure by the Bank of America."[19] Soon it was bankrupt.

*Berkeley Instruments* met a similar fate, following a depletion of its working capital "as a result of one bad contract."[20]

*National Plug Company,* a firm to reprocess scrap paper, and *Value Engineering,* a pipe fabrication company, were both approved by OEDF but decided to withdraw their applications. A member of the Oakland EDA staff in 1966 remarked, "Value Engineering was turned down when it tried to get land in the Port's industrial park— the Port didn't think that a can-crusher was aesthetic enough."

The loan to *Hyatt Hotel Corporation* was approved in June 1968, but the hotel company had not yet made a final decision on locating in Oakland.

The gloomy record of business loans was summed up in an *Oakland Tribune* headline in March 1969: "U.S. INVESTS $1,085,000 TO CREATE 43 OAKLAND JOBS."[21] It is not difficult to understand why this program in Oakland has been substantially deactivated since that time. Let us now move from the depths of depression surrounding the outcome of business loans to consider an EDA project in Oakland that actually exceeded expectations—the West Oakland Health Center.

A PROJECT THAT WORKED: THE WEST OAKLAND HEALTH CENTER

In 1968, which was not in general a banner year for the EDA in Oakland, the federal agency embarked on a project that was directly tied to poor and black people. During the latter part of 1966 a dozen women residents of West Oakland had met with a graduate student in social work, a minister from the West Oakland parish, and an area physician in an effort to improve health services in the West Oakland ghetto. In early 1967 they were incorporated as a formal organiza-tion, the West Oakland Health Council, Inc. (WOHCI). Meetings with interested professionals and official agencies led the group to

19. EDA internal report, p. 43.
20. *Ibid.,* p. 41.
21. *Oakland Tribune,* March 16, 1969, p. 1.

concentrate initially on collecting statistics to document the needs of the community.[22]

Under a grant from the Office of Economic Opportunity, the Alameda County Health Department lent the services of a health statistician to the group to assist it in designing and carrying out a health survey for a random sample of the West Oakland population. The survey showed that, although the population of West Oakland comprised only 9 percent of the population under the jurisdiction of the county health department, the West Oakland area had: 20 percent of the measles cases, 30 percent of the tuberculosis cases, 50 percent of the gonorrhea cases, and 51 percent of the syphilis cases. In addition, the infant mortality rate was considerably higher (38 per 1,000 births) in West Oakland than for the county as a whole (19.2 per 1,000 births). There were few health care specialists in the area.[23]

The local community group determined to develop a health facility, and the WOHCI was encouraged by the United States Public Health Service to apply for funding for an outpatient program. For the land and construction of the building itself, WOHCI sought help from the Oakland Redevelopment Agency. Funds were also sought from outside sources like the National Medical Association Foundation, a black medical federation. The WOHCI also anticipated funding from the Model Cities program.

The EDA's Oakland representatives at that time, Charles Patterson and Fred Ricci, had followed these events and had given assistance to WOHCI. When it appeared that the original financing from both the NMA and Model Cities was in jeopardy, the EDA officials encouraged the community group to apply for EDA public works funding. The WOHCI and the Public Health Service formally requested that the EDA provide a 60 percent grant and 40 percent loan award for the center. The WOHCI would direct administration of the center and would contract with a group of physicians—the West

22. We are indebted to Douglas G. Montgomery, who was a postdoctoral fellow in the EDA during 1969–70, for the health center chronology. See his "The Federal Delivery System: Impact on the Community. A Case Study of EDA and the West Oakland Health Center" (paper delivered at the American Political Science Association annual meeting, 1970). Montgomery carried on the study as a temporary member of EDA's Office of Policy Coordination. Approval for the study was given by Richard Sinnott in the fall of 1969.
23. *Ibid.*, p. 19.

Oakland Health Group—to provide services there. The development of the project was estimated to create one hundred new jobs; furthermore, it would serve as a training facility for medical, paramedical, and subprofessional occupations.

Early in May 1968, the Oakland EDA office sent a memorandum to Washington recommending approval of the project. There was some concern in Washington about financing arrangements, since the EDA had had no previous experience with funding a health facility that operated on the basis of a recipient's ability to pay. Some doubted that the facility could produce revenues adequate to pay the loan.[24] Furthermore, the EDA's public works experience in Oakland thus far had not been pleasant at all; the hangar and terminal projects were both stalled at the time.

In spite of these doubts, the EDA agreed to fund the project early in June 1968. The promised EDA funding totaled $1.3 million to construct the 26,000-square-foot medical center; there was to be a $650,000 grant and a $650,000 loan. Participants interviewed credit George Karras, director of the Office of Public Works, with piloting this decision through the EDA bureaucracy. Thus, the project had for an ally a man who could offer sustained and effective help in the process of implementation that lay ahead.

With the project approved, those "technical details" began to crop up again. The Public Health Service and the WOHCI had entered into negotiations with a private contractor, Designed Facilities Corporation (DFC), to work on the building. This firm had assured the WOHCI that use of prefabricated structures would save time in building; it also wanted to operate both as the architect/engineer and general contractor under a negotiated contract with the WOHCI.

The EDA is normally opposed to a procedure that allows one firm to design and construct a project; competitive bidding is the agency's rule. Nevertheless, after some disagreement, the EDA agreed to let the WOHCI deviate from normal procedure in this case. The Public Health Service was firmly behind design-and-construct, and DFC had promised to complete the facility within ninety days after starting construction.[25] By acceding to design-and-construct, the EDA

24. *Ibid.*, p. 22.
25. *Ibid.*, p. 25.

had reduced the number of necessary clearances in program implementation.

Familiar troubles surfaced in July: the contractor notified its clients that cost overruns would occur. But the EDA was committed to building the center and showing results; besides, the overrun necessitated only a $200,000 increase. So in August 1968 the EDA increased the grant and loan by $100,000 each. Douglas G. Montgomery notes: "EDA continued to push the Center because of its direct benefits to the community although the special experience of the negotiated contract to fund this project was becoming less accommodative to the agency."[26]

Further delays were caused in fall 1968 when members of the WOHCI began to disagree "over what they desired and what they could afford."[27] In early December representatives of the EDA and PHS met to discuss the delayed construction. "Both federal agencies continued to agree," Montgomery reports, "that the self determination activity by WOHCI in managing its own program was an important part of the project's operation."[28]

While EDA officials were trying to decide what to do about the terminal and hangar projects throughout spring and summer 1969, the West Oakland Health Center was taking shape. In February a contract had been signed under which Designed Facilities Corporation was the prime contractor; that company in turn designated Trans-Bay Engineering and Builders (minority builders) as its principal contractor. The contract totaled $1,004,995 for the construction of the facility and the architect/engineering services.[29]

The financing arrangements for the project's construction were somewhat unusual. Because the borrower was unable to obtain interim financing, the EDA agreed to disburse funds on a cost-incurred basis during construction. (The federal agency wanted to avoid the cost escalation that inevitably followed undue delay.) Furthermore, instead of making loan and grant disbursements to the West Oakland Health Council, the EDA paid the contractors directly. An EDA public works staff member explains the reason for

26. *Ibid.*
27. *Ibid.*
28. *Ibid.*
29. *Ibid.*

this deviation from normal practice: "There was a lot of infighting within the West Oakland Health Council. They changed their top management, and the executive director who lost out in a power struggle sued the council. Pending the suit, we thought there might have been a judgment to freeze the Council's assets, so we paid the creditors directly to keep the project going."

Several delays prevented the center from being completed by the contractor's target date of June 15, 1969. The subcontractors had some trouble finding an adequate number of competent workmen and also made mistakes in scheduling. Then problems occurred with the assembly of fixtures in the facility. Although the primary contractor had intended to install plumbing fixtures in the modules at the factory, the city of Oakland Building Department ruled that fixtures had to be installed at the site. But these problems were finally resolved, and the center was completed on August 20, 1969.[30] By December 1970 the center had provided 160 jobs—including 150 for minorities.

30. *Ibid.*, p. 26.

# 5

## The Complexity of Joint Action

INTRODUCTION

When we say that programs have failed, this suggests we are surprised. If we thought from the beginning that they were unlikely to be successful, their failure to achieve stated goals or to work at all would not cry out for any special explanation. If we believed that intense conflicts of interests were involved, if people who had to cooperate were expected to be at loggerheads, if necessary resources were far beyond those available, we might wonder rather more why the programs were attempted instead of expressing amazement at their shortcomings. The problem would dissolve, so to speak, in the statement of it. No explanatory ingenuity would be required. A trite and commonplace question would receive a self-evident answer. Even if the initiators of the programs failed to appreciate the bitter conflict they would set off, we should simply investigate their failures of perception, having thus explained the inevitable unhappy outcomes.

It is not surprising, for example, that the EDA business loans program in Oakland failed. Given contradictory legislative criteria, inherent administrative antagonisms between federal agencies, and the uncertainty of local action on the part of numerous businesses, it is no wonder that the program failed to achieve its aims. In public works, at least, the EDA had the advantage of dealing with one

PROFESSOR BUTTS GETS HIS THINK-TANK WORKING AND EVOLVES THE SIMPLIFIED PENCIL-SHARPENER. OPEN WINDOW (A) AND FLY KITE (B). STRING (C) LIFTS SMALL DOOR (D) ALLOWING MOTHS (E) TO ESCAPE AND EAT RED FLANNEL SHIRT (F). AS WEIGHT OF SHIRT BECOMES LESS, SHOE (G) STEPS ON SWITCH (H) WHICH HEATS ELECTRIC IRON (I) AND BURNS HOLE IN PANTS (J). SMOKE (K) ENTERS HOLE IN TREE (L), SMOKING OUT OPOSSUM (M) WHICH JUMPS INTO BASKET (N) PULLING ROPE (O) AND LIFTING CAGE (P), ALLOWING WOODPECKER (Q) TO CHEW WOOD FROM PENCIL (R) EXPOSING LEAD. EMERGENCY KNIFE (S) IS ALWAYS HANDY IN CASE OPOSSUM OR THE WOODPECKER GETS SICK AND CAN'T WORK.

*(Rube Goldberg cartoon from Rube Goldberg vs. the Machine Age, ed. Clark Kinnaird, New York: Hastings House, 1968, p. 18.)*

DOES IT HAVE TO BE THIS COMPLICATED?

major recipient—the Port of Oakland—and that recipient was known to have excellent management and the best credit rating. There was no question of whether the port was qualified, only if it would make good on its promises. Business loans, on the other hand, had to work through a variety of local firms, a number of whom had management of doubtful quality. And the applications had to be approved by a board of local businessmen who were critical of the whole EDA effort. The statutory criteria for eligibility of borrowers, furthermore, were both stringent and incompatible. It was difficult for a potential borrower to demonstrate that his firm would provide new employment in the area that did not compete with existing business. It was more difficult for him to show that he could not finance his proposal through private lending facilities (which meant that he was considered a poor risk), while convincing the EDA and SBA that he would not default on his loan.

Yet EDA officials in Oakland took on an additional challenge by deciding to apply the employment plan to business loans projects. A former EDA loan official in Washington commented on the effects of this decision: "You start with poor borrowers. Then the poor borrower has to hire the world's poorest work force. Then we expect him to compete with rich businessmen with experienced work forces." When the EDA loan office tried to provide a struggling Oakland businessman (who had hired some unemployed minority workers) with enough management assistance to keep his firm afloat, an EDA technical assistance officer vetoed the project. After all, reasoned the official, if the man needs all that help, he couldn't be a good businessman. EDA can lend building capital, but not working capital. Under the watchful banker's eye of the Small Business Administration, which can loan working capital, the firm eventually went bankrupt.

Faced with a numerous and needful set of participants, compelled to relate to them through a series of complex criteria, EDA officials might well have begun to long for the relative simplicity of the public works projects. Who does this sort of thing to himself? In the full flood of enthusiasm, EDA officials may not have realized what they were getting into when they joined race and poverty with business management and employment. But they did have a long legislative history to warn them that loan programs involved deeply rooted conflicts of interests. The criteria for loans, which seemed to cry out for parody, are the product of accommodation to the conflicts that arose when the federal government first discovered that it wasn't always easy to help some people without hurting others. And a further conflict had been built into the program by the requirement that the EDA and SBA—agencies whose priorities differed markedly—should share responsibility for administering the loan program.

Because of pervasive conflicts within the business loans program, its decision rules were complex; competing interests had to be taken into account. The idea that employment for minorities is good in and of itself had to give way to the desirability of limiting competition with existing firms, to allowing the Small Business Administration to deal with applicants in its domain, to not taking over the role of the private market in funding companies able to use its facilities. The very complexity of the decision rules, however, militated against their successful use since so few applicants could satisfy them. The criteria, in fact, began to scare away applicants. The men in charge of moving the money had to simplify their lives. They ended up, quite reasonably in their own terms, deciding to pick a little of this and a little of that to see what would happen. They even made a concession in the direction of local opinion by insisting on the formation of a citizens group to help appraise proposals. But it did not help local citizens to be asked to make decisions that they were not competent to make. Moreover, there was little room for choice because not many proposals came up. There is a name for that, but rubber-stamping does not somehow equal citizen participation.

When a program is characterized by so many contradictory criteria, antagonistic relationships among participants, and a high level of uncertainty about even the possibility of success, it is not hard to predict or to explain the failure of the effort to reach its goals. "When, as in the case of ESEA," Bailey and Mosher write, "a law unprecedented in scope has to be administered through State and local instrumentalities, on an impossible time schedule, by an understaffed agency in structural turmoil, beset by a deluge of complaints and demands for clarification of the legislation at hand, as well as cognate legislation already on the books; the wonder is not that mistakes are made—the wonder is that the law is implemented at all."[1]

1. Stephen K. Bailey and Edith K. Mosher, *ESEA: The Office of Education Administers a Law* (Syracuse, N.Y.: Syracuse University Press, 1968), p. 99.

We are more surprised by program failure in a case in which there is apparent agreement at the beginning, but in which disagreements soon surface to block the program. Such a case was provided by the "new towns in-town" program, which is the subject of an excellent analysis by Martha Derthick.[2] Late in the summer of 1967, the Johnson administration started a program to build model new communities on surplus federally owned land in metropolitan areas. During the next year, the White House and the Department of Housing and Urban Development announced seven projects. They were to be located in Washington, D.C., San Antonio, Atlanta, Louisville, Clinton Township (Michigan), New Bedford, and San Francisco. Nearly three years later, the program had clearly failed. Three of the projects were dead, and the rest were in serious trouble. Almost no construction had been initiated.[3]

Why would anyone want to look a gift horse in the mouth? Why would anyone reject the benevolent efforts of President Johnson, the White House, and the Department of Housing and Urban Development to offer subsidies on federally owned surplus land in metropolitan areas for the laudable purpose of building new communities joining black and white, rich and poor, living together in harmony with the new technology? Although initial agreement appeared—at least to the federal officials—to be widespread, disagreements rapidly came to the surface. A number of local groups strongly opposed low cost public housing; local officials preferred kinds of development that would yield more tax revenue; and conservationists were opposed to plans for construction. As apparent agreement rapidly yielded to pervasive disagreement, the program ground to a halt.

We could justify our surprise at program failure still better (thereby enhancing the interest in asking why programs fail) by taking a case in which initial agreements dissolved slowly over time in unpredictable ways. Antagonisms would not be evident at the beginning, nor would they emerge rapidly. Rather, the conflicts would be covert and would become evident only after some time had passed. The interests and organizations involved would have thought they wanted to do something, but experience would teach them that they had been mistaken. Few programs could be undertaken if all par-

2. Martha Derthick, *New Towns In-Town* (Washington, D.C.: Urban Institute, 1972).
3. *Ibid.*, p. xiv.

ticipants had to be specified in advance, all future differences resolved at the outset, and future bargains made under yesterday's conditions. Something has to be left to the unfolding of events. Then as latent conflicts become manifest, the original agreements have to be renegotiated and a new and possibly more antagonistic situation emerges. The federal agency may discover that its funding recipients are not willing to abide by initial agreements, or the recipients may interpret the agreements in ways that conflict with federal interpretations. An agency that appears to be a single organization with a single will turns out to be several suborganizations with different wills. The apparent solidity of original aims and understandings gives way as people, organizations, and circumstances change. So far, so good. But not good or far enough.

It could be said that the EDA public works program was characterized by the slow dissolution of agreement. As one delay succeeded another, the major individual participants changed and so did the understandings they had with one another. Agreements were reached, eroded, and remade. The frequent calls for coordination, which we shall subject to analysis in the next chapter, reflected the inability of the machinery for implementation to move fast enough to capture the agreements while they lasted. Allow enough time to elapse in a rapidly changing external world and it is hard to imagine any set of agreements remaining firm. We expect the national economy (and the position of individual firms within it) to be subject to rapid fluctuation. Why, then, should agreements made in what must seem like a bygone era retain their original binding force? Anyone can understand why agreement is subject to modification over time; everyone wants to know why it took so long to implement the public works and employment program that everybody wanted in the beginning. There is less of a challenge in explaining why agreements break down years after they have been entered into than in discovering why it is so difficult to implement them at the time they are made.

It is more interesting, we think, to maximize surprise. We have chosen to analyze the EDA public works program in Oakland precisely because it lacks those elements that permit the easy explanations. Compared, say, with community action or urban redevelopment, the EDA's involvement in Oakland lacks both drama and conflict. Unlike business loans, there were no obvious conflicting interests and contradictory legislative criteria. And unlike "new towns in-town," there was no opposition on the local level. In EDA public works, all the major participants throughout the program's history insisted that they believed in the program and that there were no fundamental disagreements among them. The happenings we record are important to us for their everyday prosaic character. These are the kinds of things—changing actors, diverse perspectives, multiple clearances—that are found in any program.

Indeed, the EDA made special efforts to overcome obstacles that were known to have hampered other programs. The EDA's innovation, from its own point of view, consisted precisely in trying to avoid the institutional fragmentation, multiple and confusing goals, and inadequate funding that had characterized previous federal-city programs. The marine terminal and airline hangar projects, on which we shall concentrate for analytical purposes, deliberately included just one federal agency in one city; there would be only one major local recipient, the Port of Oakland, whose tenants' performance would be bound by a written and signed employment plan; and there would be an immediate commitment of $23 million. The straightforward construction of job-producing public works was the heart of the EDA program for Oakland. We are unlikely to get many programs that will be simpler in that they involve fewer participants or less complicated arrangements. Few programs would specify as clearly the benefits to the participants—cheap money, jobs, political credit—than this one. The difficulties that arose here, therefore, can be expected to afflict almost any new program. If we understand why this program ran into difficulty, we can hope to get at some of the underlying factors that make programs fail when there is no apparent reason why they should.

What we hope to show is that the apparently simple and straightforward is really complex and convoluted. We are initially surprised because we do not begin to appreciate the number of steps involved, the number of participants whose preferences have to be taken into account, the number of separate decisions that are part of what we think of as a single one. Least of all do we appreciate the geometric growth of interdependencies over time where each negotiation involves a number of participants with decisions to make, whose implications ramify over time. What is so hard about building a ter-

minal and airline hangar when the money is there, the plans are
signed, and the people agree that minorities are to get a share of the
jobs? We will show that what seemed to be a simple program turned
out to be a very complex one, involving numerous participants, a
host of differing perspectives, and a long and tortuous path of decision points that had to be cleared. Given these characteristics, the
chances of completing the program with the haste its designers had
hoped for—and even the chances of completing it at all—were
sharply reduced.

## A MULTIPLICITY OF PARTICIPANTS AND PERSPECTIVES

Although the EDA had intended to carry out its program in a direct
and simple manner, without extensive participation by other government agencies, a large number of governmental and nongovernmental organizations and individuals eventually became involved in the
process of implementation. To list every participant who became
involved in some aspect of the EDA program would exhaust both us
and our readers. Let us agree, therefore, to oversimplify the situation. We shall restrict the participants to the EDA, the rest of the
federal government, and the city of Oakland, with their constituent
elements. For the EDA this would mean the initial Foley-Bradford
task force, EDA operating departments in Washington, the agency's
leadership after Foley, the regional office in Seattle, and the field
office in Oakland. Other federal agencies that became involved included the General Accounting Office; the Department of Health,
Education and Welfare; the Department of Labor; and the navy.
Participants in Oakland were the mayor, city administrators, the
Port of Oakland, World Airways, and several of the city's black
leaders, conservation groups, and tenants of the Port of Oakland.

Some of these participants (such as the departments of Labor and
Health, Education, and Welfare) became involved because they
possessed jurisdictional authority over important parts of the project; others (like the navy) entered the process when they felt their
interest being impinged on; and still others (such as black people
in Oakland) were intentionally brought into the program by the
EDA in order to build local support for the projects.

Each of the many participating groups, as Table 6 shows, had a

TABLE 6: Participants and Perspectives in the Oakland EDA Program

| Participant | Connection with Program | Perspective and Major Objectives | Sense of Urgency |
|---|---|---|---|
| EDA—Foley, Bradford, Oakland task force | Designed program, set up project machinery in Oakland | Wanted to initiate, in a relatively short time, a program of economic development which would create jobs for unemployed minorities | Very high |
| EDA—Operating departments in Washington | Project implementation —construction, financial processing, etc. | Aimed for construction of facilities in an efficient and administratively proper manner | High (some resentment of special task force; insistence that process meet administrative standards) |
| EDA—Leadership after Foley | Exercised authority over projects after fall 1966 | Sought to salvage original employment goals in Oakland project | Moderate (not personally identified with program; Secretary of Commerce Connor indicated lack of enthusiasm) |
| EDA—Seattle Regional Office | Unclear; processed paperwork, but no final authority to commit funds | Attempted to gain larger administrative role in project | Moderate |
| EDA—Oakland Office | Monitoring of projects at local level | Hoped to salvage initial employment goals and complete project | Varied with each man in office |

TABLE 6: (Continued)

| Participant | Connection with Program | Perspective and Major Objectives | Sense of Urgency |
|---|---|---|---|
| U.S. General Accounting Office | Questioned EDA policy regarding grant/loan ratio for Port projects | Concerned with standards for disbursement of federal funds | Low |
| U.S. Department of Health, Education, and Welfare | Joint control over manpower training funds for hangar project | Supported goal of job training in Oakland, but had commitment to established skills centers | Low (East Bay Skills Center bypassed by airline training program) |
| U.S. Department of Labor | Joint control over manpower training funds for hangar project | Main interest was in job training | Low |
| U.S. Navy | Objected to terminal construction because of effects on flight safety | Was chiefly concerned with effects of port construction on operations of Alameda Naval Air Station | Low |
| City of Oakland (mayor) | Represented city in dealings with EDA; tried to build support for program | Strongly supported EDA goals of economic development and job creation | High |
| City of Oakland (administration) | Drew up public works applications for EDA funding (coliseum access road approved) | Saw EDA funding as potential support for city public works projects | Low (access road completed early; no other city-sponsored projects approved) |

| | | | |
|---|---|---|---|
| Port of Oakland | Local recipient of major public works projects | Viewed EDA program as vital support for Port building program, but annoyed by multiplicity of federal guidelines | Moderate (Port is involved in building and operating numerous other facilities) |
| Oakland black leaders | Met by Foley and Bradford on early visits; some served on Employment Plan Review Board | Wanted job creation for minorities | High |
| Conservation groups | Protested Port of Oakland bay-fill activities | Strongly protested fill as damaging to bay and environs | Low |
| Port of Oakland tenants | If benefitted from EDA financing, had to sign employment agreement | Wanted to operate successful business | Low |

distinctive perspective from which it viewed the EDA operation, and the groups differed widely in their sense of urgency about the program. Even within an organizational unit, there can be substantial differences in outlook. Thus, the special EDA Oakland task force was primarily interested in the agency's making a rapid and dramatic commitment to a job program for minorities, while the operating departments in the EDA Washington office concentrated their concern on the administrative and financial soundness of project construction. Within the city government in Oakland, Mayor Reading's focus on the job-producing aspects of the program was not shared by city administrators, who saw the EDA as a possible funding source for the city government's public works.

When perspectives differ, so also do measures of success. For the original EDA leadership, the major criterion of success was the number of jobs created for minority hard-core unemployed in Oakland. But other participants had competing success criteria: the Port of Oakland was mainly interested in the expansion of its facilities, while the Department of Health, Education, and Welfare was pressing for increased funding for its established skills centers.

None of the participants seriously disagreed with the policy of developing jobs for unemployed minorities in Oakland, nor did any of them question the advisability of creating jobs through grants for public works. Why, in view of this lack of opposition to the thrust of EDA policy, did the program run into so many obstacles?

When programs are not being implemented, it is tempting to conclude that the participants disagreed about the special ends they sought rather than the ordinary means for attaining them. Thinking about means and ends in isolation, however, imposes an artificial distinction, especially when more than one program is involved. One participant's ends, such as a training facility, may be another actor's means. Once innumerable programs are in operation, the stream of transactions among people who are simultaneously involved in them may evidence neither clear beginning nor end but only an ebb and flow. As the managers of each program try to impose their preferred sequence of events on the others, their priorities for the next step, which differs for each one and cannot be equally important to all, may conflict. The means loom larger all the time because they are what the action is about. Actually, it is easier to disagree about means because they are there to provoke quarrels, while ends are always around the corner. To make concrete an otherwise abstract notion we provide a list of reasons why participants may agree with the substantive ends of a proposal and still oppose (or merely fail to facilitate) the means for effectuating it.

*(1) Direct incompatibility with other commitments.*—Participants may agree with the merits of a proposal but find that it is incompatible with other organizational goals. HEW came to view the EDA's airline training proposal as competing for scarce funds with the East Bay Skills Center, which was on HEW's own list of approved institutions. And the Port of Oakland, while expressing its support of the EDA's employment goals, still stressed the need to "market its property." A port representative remarked that "the Port's methods and EDA methods are different, but . . . their principles are the same." The port spokesman said that his organization wanted to do something for minority unemployed, but that the EDA didn't understand what it is like to put together a project and make it work. Port officials felt that EDA restrictions—particularly the employment plan—were burdensome. This judgment was concurred with by Matson Navigation Company, which did not wish to use those port facilities that were subject to the EDA employment plan.

*(2) No direct incompatibility, but a preference for other programs.*—Many EDA employees, especially those who had served in the ARA, viewed rural areas and small towns as the proper focus of the agency. This view has also been held by the federal Office of Management and Budget. These participants did not oppose the idea of creating jobs in urban areas, but they did not feel this was the EDA's task.

*(3) Simultaneous commitments to other projects.*—Participants may agree with a proposal, have no contradictory commitments, and not prefer any alternative programs, but they may have other projects of their own that demand time and attention. The Port of Oakland's architect/engineer delayed his work on plans for the marine terminal, because his staff was busy on other port projects. And World Airways wanted to develop a general building program before it settled on specific criteria for the hangar. Such delays caused displeasure at the EDA, in much the same way that the federal agency's administrative delays caused disappointment at the port.

*(4) Dependence on others who lack a sense of urgency in the project.*—In the course of implementing a project, individuals or organizations may be called on because of their expertise or jurisdictional authority. Yet they may lack a sense of urgency about the overall program. Into this category would fall the consulting engineers, who designed plans for local recipients, and the Department of Labor, whose assent was necessary to carry out the airline training program under Section 241 of the MDTA.

*(5) Differences of opinion on leadership and proper organizational roles.*—Participants who agree about a program's goals may nevertheless disagree about which people or organizational units should be running the programs. Members of EDA operating divisions resented the special status accorded to Bradford's Oakland task force, and after the departure of Foley and Bradford the whole Oakland project was treated with less urgency. Both Secretary of Commerce Connor and Foley's successor, Ross Davis, felt that the Oakland project was Foley's personal project; they did not share Foley's enthusiasm for a dramatic EDA push in urban areas. And EDA regional officials, disturbed by the direct Oakland-Washington relationship, tried to convince Oakland representatives to route funding requests through the regional office in Seattle. Differences over program leadership constituted additional reasons for delay.

*(6) Legal and procedural differences.*—Discussing the frustrations of the early days of public works program implementation, an EDA task force member remarked that

There were all sorts of technical things that had to be decided. The job issue came later. There were a number of questions about EDA policy—how you process these things, how much meddling EDA would do in that. In September, October, November of 1966, there was hostility between the EDA and the Port on construction issues. The quality of land fill, for example. . . . At every point, the Port and EDA had their own engineering opinions. There was hardening, but not over the right issues. They were fighting about land fill, but they *should* have been worrying about employment.

Taking this viewpoint, however reasonable it may appear, depends on the intensity of one's concern with employment. Another man, differently situated, with responsibilities for protecting life in and navigation on the bay, would legitimately be concerned about the kinds of materials poured into it. The same is true for the navy's interest in reducing hazards to its planes. While it is easy to pooh-pooh these concerns, a plane crash or a scandal about additional pollution in the bay would lead to severe condemnation of the responsible officials. No one then would accept the argument that the main thing a few years earlier was to facilitate minority employment by building something. A parallel way of approaching the same problem is to say that the built-in conflict between overhead organizations, such as the government accountants concerned with legality of expenditure, and line organizations, who have direct operating responsibilities, had to be worked out in this case. Accommodations between the two perspectives are important and possible but there must be an ultimate residue of conflict. After all, the purpose of overhead organizations, whether they be personnel, accounting, or whatever, is precisely to establish a check on the behavior of line officials.

The technical issues of land fill and interim financing held up the marine terminal project. In the summer of 1969, the letting of bids for filling and dredging at the terminal project was delayed by the port's attorney because of legal complications. In none of these cases was there disagreement over the basic program goal of providing employment for minorities, but procedural and legal complications caused delay nevertheless.

Although some participants were peripheral in terms of interest in the project, expressing neither agreement nor disagreement with its substantive goals, they were nevertheless able to hold up implementation when they felt their interests being impinged on. Thus, the United States General Accounting Office questioned the EDA's grant/loan policies on port projects, while the navy lodged complaints about the terminal's effect on jet flights from the nearby naval air station. These agencies may have been peripheral in terms of their interest in the project, but their concerns had to be taken seriously by the EDA.

*(7) Agreement coupled with lack of power.*—Certain participants may agree enthusiastically with a proposal, but they may lack the resources to do much to help it. Mayor Reading strongly supported the EDA job-creation program, but he lacked the political and administrative power to force other participants to move the program along. Those members of Oakland's black community who had been

contacted by EDA officials also strongly supported the program, but they had no effective role. They were the recipients of the EDA's concern, but the port was designated to receive the project funding. Both the mayor and the black leaders were EDA supporters, but their lack of resources made them peripheral to the program. Although it had aimed for simplicity, the EDA program eventually involved a large group of diverse participants. And while none of these participants expressed disagreement with the goal of providing jobs for minorities through the building of public works, this does not mean that they were ready to make the decisions, provide the clearances, and come to the agreements necessary to speed the program on its way.

### THE MULTIPLICITY OF DECISIONS AND THE
### DECREASING PROBABILITY OF PROGRAM SUCCESS

In tracing the path of decisions and clearance points in the EDA public works program, we will again oversimplify the situation. Instead of trying to isolate every decision in which a major participant had a discernible opportunity to make choices, we will concentrate on those major decision points that determined the course of the program or that had to be passed in order for the program to continue. (We shall also assume, but only for a moment, that each point of decision is independent of the others.) Table 7, which lists these decision points and identifies the participants involved in each of them, illustrates how the multiplicity of participants and perspectives combined to produce a formidable obstacle course for the program. When a program depends on so many actors, there are numerous possibilities for disagreement and delay.

We can see that, in starting the Oakland program and in determining its early course, the EDA had to make a number of important decisions: to enter the urban field in the first place; to select Oakland as the site for its urban experiment; to choose the port as the chief recipient agency within the city; and to tie construction to jobs by means of an employment plan. Some of these early decisions were hotly debated within the agency itself. There were those, for example, who felt that the EDA, as primarily a rural agency, had no business going into cities. And a number of agency officials expressed doubts about an employment plan, which they felt would be

TABLE 7: Points of Decision and Clearance Necessary for Completion of EDA Public Works Program

| Decision Points | Participants Involved | Cumulative Total of Agreements |
|---|---|---|
| 1. Decision to involve EDA in cities (fall 1965) | Eugene Foley | 1 |
| 2. Selection of Oakland as the city for experimental effort (winter 1965) | Foley, EDA Washington | 3 |
| 3. Bypassing mayor and seeking first contacts in Oakland Black community (December 1965) | Foley-Bradford, EDA Washington | 5 |
| 4. Choice of special task force as organizational form for project (January 1966) | Foley | 6 |
| 5. Selection of employment plan as mechanism for channeling jobs to unemployed (February 1966) | Bradford-Foley, EDA task force | 8 |
| 6. Selection of local recipients of public works projects (spring 1966) | Foley, EDA task force, EDA Washington | 11 |
| 7. Negotiation and approval of employment plans (April–November 1966) | EDA task force, EDA Washington, World Airways, other port tenants, Emp. Plan Rev. Board (representing poor) | 16 |
| 8. Decision to set up training program (under Section 241 of Manpower Devel. and Training Act) at World Airways, rather than at Skills Center (summer-fall 1966) | EDA task force, EDA Washington, World Airways | 19 |

TABLE 7 (*Continued*)

| Decision Points | Participants Involved | Cumulative Total of Agreements |
|---|---|---|
| 9. Agreements required for implementation of training program (1967–68) | Local MDTA Committee, mayor, State Dept. of Employment, State Dept. of Voc. Ed., Regional Office-DOL, Regional Office-HEW, Washington Office-DOL, Washington Office-HEW, Washington EDA | 28 |
| 10. Agreement required on bay fill for construction of marine terminal (summer-fall 1966) | EDA Washington, EDA consultant, Port of Oakland | 31 |
| 11. Agreement required on interim financing arrangement (summer-fall 1966) | EDA Washington, Port of Oakland | 33 |
| 12. Negotiation of conditions for World Airways' lease of hangar (summer-fall 1966) | Port of Oakland, World Airways | 35 |
| 13. Decision on port request to relocate terminal project (January-April 1967) | EDA Washington (Davis) | 36 |
| 14. Approval of A/E contracts for terminal and hangar (March, June 1967) | EDA Washington | 37 |
| 15. Approval of preliminary plans for terminal | EDA Washington | 38 |
| 16. Decision on port request for terminal project changes and loan advance (January-February 1968) | EDA Oakland, EDA Seattle, EDA Washington | 41 |

TABLE 7 (*Continued*)

| Decision Points | Participants Involved | Cumulative Total of Agreements |
|---|---|---|
| 17. Search for agreement with navy after complaint about port construction's effect on flight safety (April 1968–April 1969) | U.S. Navy, Port of Oakland, EDA Washington | 44 |
| 18. Decision required on port request for additional financing for hangar (April 1968–February 1969) | Port of Oakland, World Airways, architect/engineers, EDA Oakland, EDA Seattle, EDA Washington | 50 |
| 19. Decision required on port request for funds for revolving restaurant (April 1968–December 1969) | EDA Seattle, EDA Washington | 52 |
| 20. Agreement required on grant/loan ratios for public works projects (April 1968) | General Acctg. Office, EDA Washington | 54 |
| 21. Decision against hangar overrun; insistence on stricter employment conditions for port and World Airways (February 1969) | EDA Washington (Davis) | 55 |
| 22. Letting of contracts for dredging and filling at terminal (June 1969) | Port of Oakland, EDA Washington | 57 |
| 23. Agreement on Port of Oakland employment plan and equal employment officer (January-September 1969) | EDA Washington, Port of Oakland | 59 |

TABLE 7 (*Continued*)

| Decision Points | Participants Involved | Cumulative Total of Agreements |
|---|---|---|
| 24. Decision to oppose terminal revolving restaurant and agreement to apply financing to construction overrun (fall 1969) | EDA Washington (Podesta-Sinnott), Port of Oakland | 61 |
| 25. Selection of contractors for construction of terminal (December 1969) | Port of Oakland, EDA Oakland, EDA Washington | 64 |
| 26. Veto of port's request that one firm both design and construct hangar (February 1969) | EDA Washington | 65 |
| 27. Decision to go ahead with hangar project, but at reduced cost and with stricter employment guidelines (February 1970) | EDA Washington (Podesta-Sinnott) | 66 |
| 28. Selection of alternative architect for hangar (April 1970) | Port of Oakland | 67 |
| 29. Approval of preliminary plans and specifications for hangar (June 1970) | EDA Washington | 68 |
| 30. Letting of contracts for construction of hangar (June 1971) | Port of Oakland, EDA Washington | 70 |

difficult to enforce. Furthermore, Eugene Foley's administrative decision to expedite the program by means of a special task force was not received with complete joy by the EDA's operating departments.

Going beyond those initial difficult decisions, there were a number of points along the way at which clearance had to be received if the program was to continue. Some of these clearances were up to the EDA itself: approval of recipients' plans and architecture contracts, authorization for advances of funds, and ruling on changes in project design. Other decision points necessitated favorable clearances by numerous participants other than the EDA. The proposed training program for airline mechanics, for example, required approval by nine federal, state, and local organizational units.

In order to get by all the decision points, the program required dozens of clearance actions by a wide range of participants. In situations of high controversy and mutual antagonism, the probability that these actions would be favorable or taken in a reasonable time might be quite small. But we have ruled out this kind of drama. Instead, we shall assume the best. We shall deliberately err on the side of assuming more agreement and good will than might actually have been the case. We shall load the dice in favor of keeping the program going. Suppose, then, we take a spread of probabilities on the high side that each participant will take a favorable action at each decision point. We can try four: 80 percent, 90 percent, 95 percent, and 99 percent. (The computations for each of these probabilities are summarized in Table 8.) However you look at it, the ultimate probability of success is very low.

TABLE 8: Program Completion Doubtful Unless Level of Agreement Among Participants Is Terribly High

| Probability of Agreement on Each Clearance Point (in percent) | Probability of Success After 70 Clearances | No. of Agreements that Reduce Probability Below 50 Percent |
|---|---|---|
| 80 | .000000125 | 4 |
| 90 | .000644 | 7 |
| 95 | .00395 | 14 |
| 99 | .489 | 68 |

We conclude that the probability of agreement by every participant on each decision point must be exceedingly high for there to be any chance at all that a program will be brought to completion. On the assumption that the probability is 80 percent (see Table 8), the chances of completion are a little over one in a million after seventy agreements have been reached, and falls below the half-way mark after just four. By increasing the probability of agreement to a healthy 90 percent, we increase the ultimate likelihood of approval to something over six in ten thousand and allow seven agreements before dipping below the 50-50 mark. Moving to 95 percent increases the probability of completion to almost four in a thousand and permits fourteen moves before the chances it will fail are better than its opportunities for success. One must advance to the 99 percent level of concurrence, an extraordinary state of affairs by any calculation, to permit a healthier sixty-eight agreements to be reached before the probability of completion drops just below the half-way mark. Clearly the data here do not merely interpret themselves but require elucidation on our part.

There is no agreement among scholars on what constitutes a decision point and thus it would be difficult for us to demonstrate that there are any particular number in the case under study. We could, with no difficulty at all, double the number of decision points by shaving down our criteria of what constitutes a separable act. We have tried to err on the side of having fewer steps rather than more by reducing the number of decision points to thirty. But each one must be increased in size by the number of separate decision-makers involved. The best defense of our rough-and-ready procedure is that the results are largely insensitive to any but the most drastic (and hardly conceivable) change in the number of participants who are required to give their consent to various decisions. A glance at Table 8 will show that, until one passes beyond 95 percent probability of agreement on each issue, only fourteen separate clearances are required to reduce the probability of completion below equality. If there is 95 percent probability of favorable action at each point, and we assume only thirty clearance points—an unrealistically low number—the probability of overall program success is .215. If there are fifty such points, the overall probability of completion drops to barely 1 percent.

By emphasizing the conflicts within each of the major participants as well as among them, we can easily lower the probabilities of agreement. Or we could try to assess the degree of urgency and commitment manifested by each participant and raise or lower its probability of favorable action on that basis. But we have already decided to give the benefit of the doubt to program success.

The high probability of agreement at each step required to produce a modest probability of successful completion makes it unnecessary to know the precise probability for any particular one. No doubt the probabilities vary from one participant and organization to another, over time within the same organization, and between different levels of government and private *versus* governmental actors. But if one assumes the best—and 99 percent for each and every clearance point appears to be about as close as one can go without assuming away the problem entirely—the odds are still against program implementation.

The computational and political problems are similar. Do we consider each participant as a separate entity, so that the final probability is simply the product of the probabilities of favorable action by each participant? Or do we show that the probabilities are linked, so that a favorable response at an early time increases the likelihood of a similar response at a later time? In political (as well as statistical) language, we are asking whether each participant is independent. To what extent is it controlled by others and to what extent can it determine its own position? Turning the question around, we ask how powerful the participant is in relation to an issue. Does an action on its part increase the probability that others will agree where they might not have done so? The most reasonable assumption in the American context of fragmented power is certainly independence of the participants. In that case, the ultimate probability of success is terribly low. If we alter the assumption to say that the federal participants are expected to follow the leadership of the EDA, so that the probability of success within the federal camp is enhanced, we are still left with the obvious fact that it cannot control local bodies. The most likely outcome at the federal level is that, seeing no great reason to oppose the central EDA position, the other participants take out degrees of opposition by delay. If we postulate that there is not only conflict but common interest between the federal and local participants, as is manifestly the case, then we would expect delay and a mixed pattern of agreement depending on how they saw their interests from one period to the next. Consequently, we can argue that, while ultimate agreement is possible but by no means certain, considerable delay is probably inevitable.

Our normal expectation should be that new programs will fail to get off the ground and that, at best, they will take considerable time to get started. The cards in this world are stacked against things happening, as so much effort is required to make them move. The remarkable thing is that new programs work at all.

Program decisions, of course, do not always consist of clear-cut "yes" or "no" responses. Programs can be delayed, modified, scaled down, and otherwise adapted or distorted to fit their environment. The possibilities will be considered shortly. Now we wish to delve into the unexpected happenings that reduce the small prospects of program implementation still further.

We have seen that, given a large number of clearance points manned by diverse and independent participants, the probability of a program achieving its goals is low. But in the case of the EDA program, we cannot merely calculate overall probability of success by taking the product of individual decision probabilities. For this program should not be viewed as a single string of green lights, all of which had to go on for the program to achieve its objectives. The situation has been more complicated than that. Given multiple program goals, there were really two distinct strings of decisions involved. And within each of these strings, we should make a distinction between those decisions that moved the project in the direction of its goal and those that were unplanned diversions from that path.

## TWO GOALS AND TWO DECISION PATHS

Rather than moving in a direct line to one goal, the EDA program aimed at achieving two major objectives: the construction of public works and the creation of jobs for the hard-core unemployed. In connection with the job-creating objective, the EDA proposed to implement a training program to prepare the hard-core unemployed to take the jobs that were opened for them. Figure 2 illustrates the two decisional sequences, as envisioned by the EDA, that would lead to the desired goals. Although the federal agency insisted initially that the two goals must be achieved together, there was always the possibility that one string of actions would be completed while the other was stalled. It is true that the employment plan tried to link construction of projects to job creation at the local level, but a crucial element of the employment strategy—the training program—was organizationally quite distinct from the rest of the program activity. The federal and state participants in that program—HEW, Labor Department, California Department of Employment—were not involved in other elements of the EDA Oakland effort, and they had no reason to share its urgency. When implementation of the training program proved impossible to effect in 1968, therefore, a key ele-

CONSTRUCTION                    EMPLOYMENT

| EDA goes into cities | | Decision to utilize employment plan |

Oakland chosen as site — Negotiation of employment plans with employers

Selection of recipient — Decision to set up training program

World Airways leases hangar — Implementation of training program

Approval of A/E contract

Approval of preliminary plans

Let contracts for dredging

Approval of construction contract

Complete construction ⟷ Jobs created and people trained

FIGURE 2. The EDA aims for two goals and sets up two paths of decisions

ment of the employment strategy was lost. Had the airline hangar been finished on schedule and had World Airways created jobs, there still would not have been the supply of trained mechanics that the EDA had counted on.

At the outset, the EDA had stated that the goals of construction and employment would go hand in hand. But as time passed and the training program became hopelessly stalled, there was pressure within the agency to concentrate on getting the construction completed. After all, a spending agency has to keep moving money and building projects or Congress will suspect that it is not doing its job. "As time goes on" an EDA official noted, "it gets harder and harder for EDA to take a tough line. We're under pressure to finish the project, and it begins to look bad for the agency if we don't. So there's great temptation to soften our demands." With frustration over mounting delays, there was always the possibility that goal displacement would occur and that the construction objective would stand alone at the EDA. But under Ross Davis and again under Robert Podesta, the agency forcibly reasserted its determination to meet both construction and employment goals. The two initial objectives were preserved, but so was the need to complete two separate strings of decisions that were each becoming longer all the time.

### THE EMERGENCE OF UNEXPECTED DECISIONS

Not only was it necessary to complete two decision paths in order to achieve the EDA program goals; but within each path, the agency found that the number of decisions and clearances required was constantly growing. Figure 2, p. 111, showed the clusters of decisions that the EDA expected would lead to the completion of the program. But Figure 3 illustrates how a large number of unexpected decisions and clearance points eventually became part of project implementation. These decisions had not been part of the EDA's plans, and they did not advance the program directly toward the achievement of its objectives. Nevertheless, they were necessary to clear blockages and enable the program to move on. The result was the emergence in each decision path of numerous diversions not intended by the program sponsors.

The paths of required decisions, as we can see, were soon characterized by more unexpected elements than expected ones: they were anything but straight lines leading directly to goals. And in one case —the failure to implement the airline training program—a decision path had been broken at a crucial point. Furthermore, the diagram in Figure 3 does not—and cannot—show a completed program. For as this is written, total project construction has not yet been completed and the job-creation process lies in the future. There will doubtless be more surprises to come.

What had looked like a relatively simple, urgent, and direct program—involving one federal agency, one city, and a substantial and immediate funding commitment—eventually involved numerous diverse participants and a much longer series of decisions than was planned. None of the participants actually disagreed with the goal of providing jobs for minority unemployed, but their differing perspectives and senses of urgency made it difficult to translate broad substantive agreement into effective policy implementation. It was not merely the direction of their decisions—favorable or unfavorable—but the time orientation of the participants—fast or slow, urgent or indolent—that determined the prospects of completion. When so many future decisions depend on past actions, delay in time may be equivalent to defeat in substance.

### THE ANATOMY OF DELAY

Expectations about new governmental programs violate common, everyday experience. People who regularly deal with inanimate objects such as computer programs would never expect a new one to run the first time. "Debugging" is not something done on the rare occasion when things go wrong but is an expected part of making a program work. Numerous iterations, extending over long periods of time, may be required before the new program performs adequately. The wise man, who knows that implementing the program will require a substantial investment though he cannot quite predict how much, will at least make an informal calculation that the likely benefits are worth the effort. Failure to implement the program in a short time, working under imposed deadlines, would not surprise him. He is merely fortunate that, hidden from public view, he is less likely to be taken to task for lack of results. And the machine will not make speeches about how he has abused it.

Appearances are deceiving. Looking back at the very array of governmental programs that are in operation, we conclude that they must have been implemented. Why, then, should our new program fail in implementation when so many others that fill the landscape have evidently succeeded? It is easy to forget (perhaps be-

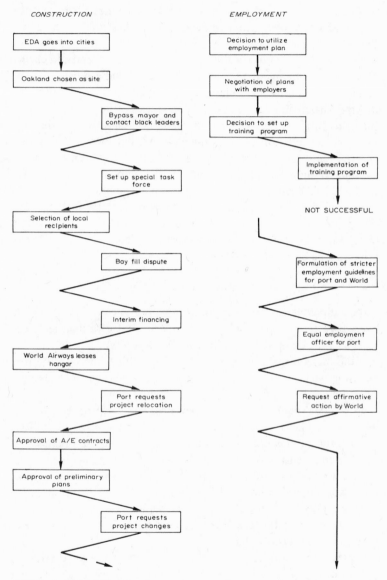

FIGURE 3. Unexpected developments cause divergences in decision paths

CONSTRUCTION                    EMPLOYMENT

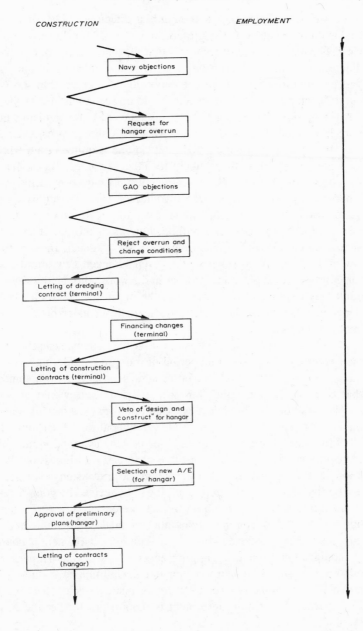

cause we never knew) about their initial difficulties. The years of trial and error that led to the present state of operation are lost from view. The huge amount of resources that may have been poured into different alternatives before one caught on is conveniently part of past history for which we are not responsible. Programs that started out to accomplish one set of objectives end up accomplishing another for which, long after the fact, we give undue credit for implementation. Everything that exists must have some consequences, even if they are not the ones anticipated or if no one is quite certain what they are. Every program is likely to affect someone, somewhere, sometime. Adaptation to the environment must have been achieved; otherwise, by definition, programs would not exist. No genius is required to make programs operative if we don't care how long they take, how much money they require, how often the objectives are altered or the means for obtaining them are changed. Indeed, the law of averages would suggest that, given sufficient new initiatives, some of them must grow and prosper in the world, though the flawed adult may bear scant resemblance to the promising child. Our task is not to romanticize the past but to learn from its errors how to improve the future.

A basic reason programs survive is that they adapt themselves to their environment over a long period of time. In considering the sequence of events necessary to implement a program, we assumed that at each decision point the various participants would give a simple "yes" or "no." While this assumption may be met by some participants part of the time, it would rarely hold for all participants all of the time. However useful an all-or-nothing assumption may be to begin analysis, it is clearly insufficient to end our discussion. We know that a negative act by a participant at a decision point need not signify that the program is dead; it can be revived by going back later on and seeking a favorable verdict. Vetoes are not permanent but conditional. Accommodations may be made, bargains entered into, resistances weakened. The price of ultimate agreement is delay or modification of the existing program. Let us see what happens to our original analysis when we alter our assumption to include the possibility that numerous attempts may be made to secure clearances from participants whose agreement is required to further the program.

For present purposes, each actor's relationship to a program may be characterized along three dimensions. What is the direction of his preference on the matter at issue? Is he for or against? What is his intensity of preference? Does he care a lot about it, or is he relatively indifferent? What resources can he bring to bear to affect the outcome? Is he strong or weak? In regard to resources, we really want to know not how strong a participant is in general, but how much of his available resources he is willing to commit to influence a particular program. We can, therefore, without prejudicing the analysis, make the simplifying assumption that use of resources is a direct function of intensity of preference. Those who manifest high intensity will use up resources to control outcomes, and those with low intensity will not. Table 9 shows how the differing types of relationships among these participants would lead to varying amounts of delay.

TABLE 9: Delay

| | Intensity | |
| Direction | High | Low |
| --- | --- | --- |
| Positive | 1. minimal delay, no bargaining | 2. minor delay, no bargaining |
| Negative | 4. maximal delay, bargaining over essentials | 3. moderate delay, bargaining over peripherals |

Participant 1 shows a positive direction and high intensity. He gives his consent immediately if not sooner. Participant 2 likes the program, but it does not matter much to him. It will have to wait its turn on his desk, but he will act affirmatively after a minor delay for processing. Although participant 3 evaluates the program (or the part that affects him) negatively, he is not terribly interested in it. A moderate delay can be expected during which time he bargains with the directors over peripheral aspects of the program. When he is satisfied or bought off in some other way, the program can continue to the next step. Maximal delay occurs when a participant is negative and feels strongly about his opinion. Depending on the amount of resources at his disposal, he will try to block the program unless basic concessions are made. Participant 4 may be capable of extending maximal delay into a permanent end.

Delay, then, is a function of the number of decision points, the number of participants at each point, and the intensity of their preferences. The EDA employment program was not characterized by the presence of participants with intensely negative views. Hence, it was not forced back to the beginning. But it was noteworthy for the presence of substantial numbers of minor and moderate delay types. While no one delay stands out from the others as excessive, the combination of delays has kept the program from realizing its potential.

Suppose we were to say that during the years covered by our study, 1966 through 1970, there were no maximal delay participants and that the other three types were equally divided among the actors who at one time or another were required to give their assent. How much delay would take place? Each clearance represents a potential for delay. We must, therefore, count each participant not once but every time his consent is required. Thus we begin with 70 clearances. Arbitrarily assigning a value of one week for minimal delay, three weeks for minor delay, and six weeks for moderate delay, we come up with a total of 233-1/3 weeks. (One week for each minimal delay equals 23-1/3, three weeks for each minor delay equals 70, and six for each moderate delay equals 140.) Under these assumptions the delay thus far would come out to approximately four and a half years, which is not far off the mark.

Now wait a minute. We still have not taken into account two aspects of real-life situations that affect the amount of delay. It is possible for several clearances to be sought during the same time period, thus reducing the total delay involved. At each decision point several clearances can be received simultaneously. Thus the appropriate number, given this assumption, would not be the 70 clearances but the 30 decision points. Yet it is also the case that failure to reach agreement the first time need not necessarily be fatal to a program because the parties can and do try again. We must consider the necessity of engaging in several rounds of negotiations, if not with all participants, at least with those inclined to moderate delay.

Here's how our calculations would look when we take these two new factors—simultaneous clearances and multiple, repeated negotiations—into account. Our starting number is made up of the 30 decision points. Again we allot one week for minimal delay, three weeks for minor delay, and six weeks for moderate delay. Hence there would be ten weeks taken up by the minimal and thirty by the minor delay types, as the assent of numerous participants was sought and achieved at the same time. But we must now consider that, say, three negotiating sessions will be required for each of the 10 moderate delay participants, leading to a delay on their part of 180 weeks (10 participants times six weeks delay times three rounds of negotiations apiece). Total delay is 220 weeks, which is a few months over four years.

Anyone can play this numbers game and make the totals come out as he wishes. We do not (and the reader should not) place any credence in these specific numbers. We have set aside, we believe, too little time for each type of delay, but we would rather err on the conservative side. The total delay of some four years is too low, possibly because no one, however favorably inclined, can really make a decision in a single week. Or perhaps we have discovered something about the dedication that characterized EDA officials in expediting this program as best they could. We hope to have illustrated, however, the kinds of variables that should go into theories that intend to explain delay in governmental programs.

Now we are in a position to make the analysis more complicated by reintroducing the resource variable. We can omit most of the relationships from Figure 4 because we have previously considered them. Those participants, for instance, who are positive in direction,

FIGURE 4. Delay (expanded version)

high in intensity, and strong in resources, lead to minimal delay; and those with the opposite characteristics to maximal obstruction. The participants characterized by the negative direction, high intensity, and weak resources might be interesting, but none appeared in our study. We wish, therefore, to concentrate on those who are positive in feeling about the program, strong in resources that might be committed or opposed to it, but low in intensity. Several of the potential employers of minorities may have fallen into this category. They liked the idea of minority employment—or at least they appreciated the prospect of low-cost financing—but they were not intensely committed. Had they been opposed from the start, to be sure, they would not have gotten involved in the first place. Once they decided to take part, however, their enthusiasm waned. Another way of putting it would be to say that we have located the essential policy problem: how to provide incentives to change low to high intensity or, more accurately, how to maintain high positive intensity through lengthy delays. We have treated intensity as a constant. For all but the most devoted participants, however, it is a variable. The longer the delays, the more time for intensity to decay.

The argument can be displayed graphically. Delay, as we have conceived it, as a function of resources, intensity, and direction of interest. Since "direction," that is, support or opposition, is a dichotomous variable, we can draw two sets of curves to illustrate its relationships with the other forces in the field. We would expect, from the nature of our argument, the form of the curves and the spread among them to appear as indicated in Figure 5. When resources are held constant, for instance, delay decreases with positive intensity of interest; when intensity is held constant, delay decreases with a greater commitment of resources. The shape of the curves suggests that there are diminishing returns to the application of either in-

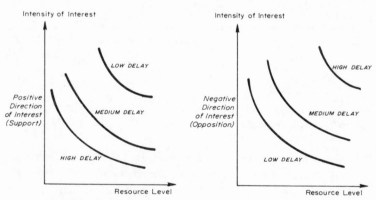

FIGURE 5. Delay as a function of direction of interest, intensity of interest, and commitment of resources

tensity or level of resources. There are also diminishing returns to scale in the sense that expanding each variable in proportion (doubling, say, resources and intensity) will not affect the amount of delay.

"Time is money," the old saw goes. "Delays are lost opportunities" might be a modern equivalent. It is worth spending a little time applying our model of delay more closely to the EDA experience in Oakland. Time is a scarce resource for men and for organizations. If you want to know what a man loves, observe how he spends his time. If you want to know what matters most to an organization, chart the activities on which its members spend their precious allotment of hours. The allocation of time deserves, though it does not receive, the same attention that we give to the allocation of financial resources.

By focusing on the policy that interests us most at a given moment, we tend to gloss over the temporal dimensions of the problem that produce so many of the difficulties that we experience. As years pass, we fail to recall the sense of time that motivated the policy in which we are interested. We would not, for instance, question the lack of a developed experimental design if we recalled that the policy was created in a few weeks and the decisions made in less than nineteen days. Care in formulation and speed in execution may be incompatible if the two are telescoped together. It is easy to ignore the fact that the sense of urgency manifested by the observer may differ from that of the participant and that, indeed, the participants may differ widely in the time and hence importance that they allocate to the program in question. We must ask whether the problem was central or peripheral. If it was central, we must also know how many other things of major importance the participant had to do at the same time. If it was peripheral, we want to know how far down in his time priorities it actually went. Even where participants agree about the merits of a program, they may still conflict over the time priority each one is to give to it. Multiply the number of participants, give them varying degrees of centrality, arrange their time budgets differently, and you have set up a typical pattern of stop and start characterized by a little forward movement and a lot of delay. We can make this analysis more concrete by illustrating the various causes of the innumerable delays that afflicted the EDA employment program in Oakland.

Not all the delays were unplanned, accidental occurrences; some were caused intentionally by participants who wanted to stop an undesired action or to step back and reassess the development of the program. Blocking delays, or purposeful halts in the process, occurred when the EDA objected to the port's bay fill in 1966 and when the agency turned down the port's request to have one firm design and construct the hangar in 1970. Delays for reassessment were ordered by the EDA in considering the port's request for the hangar overrun in 1968–69 and by the new Republican administration in order to reevaluate the entire Oakland program in 1969. In addition, procedural delays were caused by the routing of plans and funding requests through the regional office; by 1968 the EDA was searching for a useful role for its field representatives.

A number of delays resulted from alternative time priorities. No one specifically ordered these delays; they were caused by the fact that participants had other things to do at the time. The EDA's eleven-month delay in giving the port an answer on the hangar overrun request reflected the lowered priority of the Oakland project within the agency. There was a flurry of activity in 1966, followed by lengthy periods of inactivity. Participants did not turn flatly against the project, but they had other things to do. The port and World Airways had other commercial ventures to draw their attention; the EDA had hundreds of public works projects to supervise; and other federal agencies had numerous manpower projects to approve and to fund. After the departure of Foley and Bradford, the EDA cared less intensely about riding constant herd on the Oakland program. No one planned these delays, but they occurred anyway.

Program delay is often difficult to distinguish from program failure. If a favorable decision is made but it is made after a delay of years, does this count as success or failure? The answer to this question depends in large measure on the criteria that the sponsors of a program set for themselves. In the case of the EDA program in Oakland, speed was felt to be essential. Eugene Foley argued eloquently that the need for creating jobs was urgent and that immediate action was needed. In a 1966 speech Foley said,

Good grief! How many riots do we need in how many cities in this country to sink the point home that our programs for the ghetto cannot all be aimed in the long run? . . . The Negro's sounds of "NOW!" are not irrational demands or threats; they are a cry of desperation, a plea for help. . . . The heart of the problem is Negro unemployment. Jobs are the great need in a land where people are judged by what they do. . . . Unless jobs are provided, . . . jobs of dignity, jobs with career possibilities, . . . all (other) programs are practically futile.[4]

In the light of this high standard—the creation of jobs for black people *now*—delay constitutes failure. But others may reasonably argue the maxim "Better late than never."

The same problem emerges in a different form in attempting to determine the probability that a program will succeed. If decisions are not taken as rapidly as planned, if a program takes five or ten years to implement, how can we determine whether the program has succeeded? If we don't know whether or to what degree success has been achieved, we certainly cannot estimate the probability of achieving that nonexistent status. For many reasons—the existence of separate decision paths, the constant diversion of unexpected decisions that branched from each path, and the difficulty of saying whether delay constitutes failure—it would be very difficult to calculate in advance the probability of a program's success, even if we knew the probability of a favorable decision at each individual point. We are like travelers who are asked to meet people we do not know at times we cannot say and in places where the road maps take the form of mazes.

To what degree are our findings about the problems of implementation applicable to other federal programs involving localities? The EDA public works program is a bedrock example: almost any other one we could think of would involve a greater conflict over ultimate ends or more public dispute, less adequate resources in view of the end contemplated, and other features that make it evident why programs fail. We have argued, therefore, that the problems of implementation found in the Oakland program are likely to be found in other cases that occur under less favorable circumstances. An empirical demonstration would, of course, be preferable to a hypothetical one. We are hampered in this respect because we have been unable to locate relevant research. None that we know of attempts to deal with the problems posed by long sequences of decisions involving multiple participants, each dependent on what has gone before

---

4. Quoted in Amory Bradford, *Oakland's Not for Burning*, pp. 2–3.

and unable either to control the others or to predict the probability of successful outcomes at succeeding points, or even to be certain what those points will be or where their branches will lead.

But the EDA public works program did not spring ready-made out of the void. It was part of the spirit of its times. It emerged against a background of structural features—separate institutions (the federal government and the cities), each fragmented internally, seeking to cooperate in pursuit of immediate social objectives. There are relevant comparisons, both domestic and foreign, to the huge gulf between the syndrome of glorious aims and ignoble results that flow from these conditions.

# 6

## Learning from Experience

The individual who fails to learn from experience is forever lost in a chaotic world. He repeats his errors. Worse still, he has no way of navigating among the rocks and shoals of life. One direction is as good or as bad as another. He can make no sense out of his world because he is unable to use his past experience to do better in the future.

Organizations, which deal with the collective efforts of men, are devoted to the processing of information and the generation of knowledge. Their ability to test the environment so as to correct error and reinforce truth makes them effective. Inability to learn is fatal. Yet learning is more difficult because so many men must do it together. A major criticism that can be made of the EDA public works program in Oakland is that it closed off the possibilities of learning. Far from being a model from which the organization could learn success, it was not even an experiment from which the organization could learn from failure.

### WHEN AN EXPERIMENT ISN'T

Our assumptions about new public programs are far removed from reality. We assume that the people ostensibly in charge can predict the consequences of their actions, and that is often not the case. Since a problem exists, we assume that there must be a solution and that it is embodied in the program. Knowledge connecting the activities of government with desirable results in society must exist, we reason, for a program to be established. Hopes and prayers, the general desire to do good without knowing how, would seem to us frail reeds on which to lean, though these are the bases on which many programs are begun. When there is a clamor for action that must be satisfied, however, any plausible course of action must do.

Should lack of knowledge be admitted and the program emerge as a so-called experiment, we like to think that the activities involved must be so arranged that the people who run them can learn from their errors. But learning from experience is not easy. Experimental design requires a high level of sophistication and attention to detail, factors often in short supply. One would need to know what the world would have been like without the intervention and one would need to gauge its precise impact on the world apart from the other multitudinous influences working at the same moment. The very notion of discovering whether a new venture will work suggests, albeit falsely, that there is time to work out an experimental design for interpreting events in the world.

A major reason for the shortcomings of the EDA Oakland operation was its false characterization as an urban experiment. The EDA's ability to address the problems of the core cities was to be demonstrated to the world in a brief, dramatic, and highly publicized venture. The idea of a social experiment has considerable appeal, but no worthwhile experiment can be carried out in an environment where all decisions and procedures are determined by a rule of "minimum delay." The most powerful single decision rule was: "Given that there is a requirement to spend $23,000,000 in four months, select those projects which can be processed in the least time." Very little research and no experimentation could be carried on in the short time available. The decision rules actually followed (see Figures 6 and 7) are of the simplest sort imaginable.

The dictation of action by urgency means that little can be learned from analyzing the rules that led to these decisions being made. If we learn that the agency chose to fund project X simply because it had no time to search for or evaluate projects Y and Z, then we have learned little about how one might better choose between projects X, Y, and Z in the future. This is no way of turning bad experience to good use.

FIGURE 6. The public works decision tree (during initial phase)
(figure by Owen McShane)

RULES: SELECT THE TWO BEST CHECKERS.
(THERE ARE NO AVAILABLE CRITERIA AS TO WHAT
MAKES ONE CHECKER "BETTER" THAN ANOTHER)
TIME TO COMPLETE SELECTION — 0.5 SECONDS

FIGURE 7. An analogue of the EDA selection game, initial phase
(figure by Owen McShane)

Here we have touched a sensitive nerve. Our concern with the difficulties encountered by numerous programs aimed at alleviating poverty in recent years is not merely that they are often unsuccessful. We expect that there will be a degree of initial disappointment.

Public unease stems rather from the feeling that, collectively, we have not learned from failure, leaving us not only as poor but as puzzled as we were before. Even if the nature of EDA's "experiment" makes it difficult for us to learn how to choose new public works projects, one might hope that a study of the program's administrative difficulties would provide clues to the creation of better organizational designs in the future. The conditions we described in the EDA public works program are familiar to the most casual student of administration—obstruction, delay, red tape, overlapping, duplication, vacillation, hesitation. Before exploring further the nature of the organizational problems involved, we must first deal with two widely espoused administrative remedies: going outside the bureaucracy and coordination. The first remedy was actually attempted by the EDA in this case, and the second is often suggested as a cure for the kind of institutional fragmentation and competition that has characterized the program. But we will show that attempts to circumvent the bureaucracy often create more problems than they solve. And as for coordination, on closer examination we will see that it is a term not for solving problems but for renaming them so they emerge at the end the same as they were at the beginning. These nostrums are not only misleading, but their quick espousal tends to block deeper consideration of the nature of organizational difficulties, thus impairing the learning process.

## GOING OUTSIDE THE BUREAUCRACY

The first temptation is to establish a new organization. This way you can hire new people, establish your own rules, and work out patterns of operation you believe will facilitate the new activities. Since the point is to get special treatment, establishing the new organization in the White House or the Executive Office of the president is often considered. The number of outfits that can be located in this high station, however, is limited by the time and attention the president and his staff are able to devote to them. In order to conserve their time and energy, the president and his aides must normally limit severely the number of agencies reporting directly to the chief executive. Unless the president has a very special interest in an organization (including the willingness to be blamed for its errors), he will ordinarily resist taking it on. Besides, the sponsors of the new agency may not always welcome close White House scrutiny.

The next alternative in the search for organizational freedom is existence as an independent commission or semi-independent board. Such agencies report to Congress (meaning a subcommittee or two or no one at all). Their terms of office and appointment are circumscribed by numerous qualifications. The price for this sort of independence usually includes a plural form of executive, which is an open invitation for a diversity of interested parties to demand representation. The result may be watering down of the original ideas, internal conflicts, and worst of all the very delays that independence sought to avoid. The popularity of boards and commissions, moreover, has begun to wane because existing bodies are often not in high repute. The boards tend to insist on judicializing their procedures, leading to endless hearings and interminable delays, followed in important cases by long drawn-out legal battles. The affected interests, it also appears, have a way of capturing commissions largely because, over time, they are the ones who care the most. The cost of independence from ordinary bureaucratic constraints turns out to be loss of contact with the very political forces necessary to preserve the thrust of the organization.

If formal independence is rejected, it is still possible for a would-be organization to be born as a new bureau rather than as part of an established agency. A new bureau in an old department is, it appears, something of a mixed bag. A new bureau may have more autonomy in selecting personnel and establishing procedures than it would as part of an existing organization, but it is also subject to departmental regulations on all these matters. Life for departmental officials is easier if they can treat all their agencies in similar fashion; each exception is a headache increasing workload and decreasing the ability to rely on past experience. The question must also arise concerning why the new bureau should be able to circumvent civil service regulations for hiring, Budget Bureau rules for spending, comptroller general specifications for accounting, and on and on. Since the new bureau must deal with its department and possibly other bureaus, it will be under pressure to conform to their ways of doing business. The very act of repeatedly asking for exceptions may exhaust the élan of the new bureau and wear out the patience of other agencies with whom it must deal. Each exception has to be justified; each concession represents a favor that may have to be returned, a claim on future resources. Following routine procedure is just doing your job; acting outside its boundaries means doing a favor. Unless one believes the flow of favors can continuously move in a single direction they must be returned and not always in ways the new bureau would like.

The creation of new bureaus is also beset with difficulties similar to those encountered in getting started within the White House. Department heads may wish to cut back on the proliferation of new organizations. The scheduling of their work is made more difficult and the demands on their time rise with the increase in the number of organizations that account to them, whose special problems they must become aware of and whose personnel they must come to know. They fight new organizations, if only because they prefer known evils. They have a stake in existing patterns because they have learned about them. The time for change is when they arrive. But department heads rarely know enough to initiate change at the outset. After they have come, each new arrangement takes its toll in time, energy, knowledge, and adaptability.

The advantages of being new are exactly that: being new. They dissipate quickly over time. The organization ages rapidly. Little by little the regulations that apply to everyone else apply also to it. Accommodations are made with the other organizations in its environment. Territory is divided, divisions of labor are established, favors are traded, agreements are reached. All this means that the new organization now has settled into patterns of its own which it defends against interruption. Youth has gone and middle age has come, hopefully more powerful, certainly more experienced, inevitably less innovative.

The category of greatest empirical interest to us—the establishment of special arrangements, special preferences, special personnel to free an operation from the usual internal bureaucratic constraints —we have left for last. One way of establishing priority among programs is to give one of them preference in time and attention up and down the line. The head of the organization sets up a special unit in his office. He hires the people himself or at least the subordinate in charge of its operations. He gives its personnel and activities privileged access to him; it has first call on his time. Normal rules for hiring, clearing, and consulting are suspended for this program.

Immediately problems arise. If the special arrangements are so good, the other members of the organization say, they would like to share in them. They could do a few things too, they observe, if released from the ordinary constraints. They can think of some interesting ventures they might engage in so long as they too are not held strictly accountable (or held as little accountable as the privileged unit). They resent special treatment for others. Consequently, they are not enthusiastic about the privileged operation, and its success is not high on the priority list of other organizational actors. There was evidence of considerable resentment of the EDA Oakland task force on the part of other agency members in public works.

Efforts to circumvent the bureaucracy are often, in current public discussion, linked to decentralization. Whereas bureaucracy connotes red tape, decentralization bespeaks getting things done. Where bureaucracy suggests the verb "to stultify," decentralization bespeaks more admirable action words: to energize, to liberate from rigidity. To decentralize is apparently to debureaucratize.

But what happens when rival orthodoxies conflict? As we have met them in our tale of woe in Oakland, the decentralization and debureaucratization movements were at loggerheads. The Western Area Office, a decentralized field unit which officially opened in July 1966, wanted a voice in what happened in Oakland—which was in its territory. After all, the field offices were supposed to be closest to the people in a given region. But the nonbureaucratic Oakland task force did not take kindly to the initiative of the area office. Members of the task force were impatient with questions raised—and demands for authority made—by a regional office that had not been involved in the initial development of the project and that lacked any special expertise connected with it. For the task force, which was linked directly to the head of the organization, the regional office was not a manifestation of a noble principle; rather, it represented another irritating delay of the sort they once thought they had a mandate to avoid, undercut, or circumvent.

The idea of creating a nonbureaucracy within a bureaucracy was strictly a one-time short-run theory. No one expected it to last. It was designed to get something done in a hurry, after which it would presumably be all right for events to take their usual course. But that very short-run orientation—get in fast, get the job done, move out, turn it over to the bureaucrats—suggests an orientation to time that is unlikely to coincide with the requirements of a program designed to make a permanent and significant decrease in minority employment. The in-and-out perspective also speaks to the personal orientation of the key men involved: antibureaucratic men are unlikely to stick around long enough to shepherd the implementation of their program after it is started.

Racial discrimination has existed in America for over three hundred years, and the consequences of racism have left their indelible mark on the differing life chances of black and white in this country. Whatever their proximate causes, the race revolts that began with Watts are rooted squarely in history. All this suggests that it will take a lot of concentrated effort and a long time to eradicate poverty and racism. "Turning around Oakland," or turning around any American city, is something that cannot be accomplished overnight, no matter how dramatic the program. Imagination is needed, but so is perseverance.

Participants in the initial EDA Oakland effort talk about the early days in 1966 as exciting and exhilarating. Task force members worked hard to get the money to Oakland. They were diligent in setting up the employment plan and negotiating with employers. Whatever else can be said, they got the program going. Agreements were signed, public proclamations made, and intentions of future cooperation expressed. But that stage—the point at which Foley and Bradford left—was just the beginning of the story we have chronicled here.

When one lists the steps involved in setting up federal programs, one usually starts with the administration's proposal of a measure, followed by congressional approval and then commitment of funds. But the EDA Oakland experience suggests that these steps constitute only the tip of the iceberg and that a tortuous and frustrating path of implementation may lie below the surface. The creation of an antibureaucratic unit and the concerted efforts of nonbureaucratic men may be able to get a program launched; but as we have seen, launching is not enough.

If one wishes to assure a reasonable prospect of program implementation, he had better begin with a high probability that each and every actor will cooperate. The purpose of bureaucracy is precisely to secure this degree of predictability. Many of its most criticized features, such as the requirement for multiple and advance clearances and standard operating procedures, serve to increase the ability of each participant to predict what the others will do and to smooth over differences. The costs of bureaucracy—a preference for procedure over purpose or seeking the lowest common denominator—may emerge in a different light when they are viewed as part of the price paid for predictability of agreement over time among diverse participants. The price may be too high, but the cost of accomplishing little or nothing otherwise must be placed against it.

## COORDINATION

If we agree that merely circumventing the bureaucracy is not a panacea for program woes, then we must look elsewhere for organizational solutions. No phrase expresses as frequent a complaint about the federal government as does "lack of coordination." No suggestion for reform is more common than "what we need is more coordination." The EDA's traumatic experience in Oakland has certainly had its share of obstruction and delay. Yet when an evil is recognized and a remedy proposed for as long and as insistently as this one has been, the analyst may wonder whether there is not more to it.[1]

The word "coordination" has a deceptively simple appearance. Policies should be mutually supportive rather than contradictory. People should not work at cross-purposes. The participants in any particular activity should contribute to a common purpose at the right time and in the right amount to achieve coordination. A should facilitate B in order to achieve C. From this intuitive sense of coordination, however, two important and possibly contradictory meanings emerge. Participants in a common enterprise may act in a contradictory fashion because of ignorance; when informed of their place in the scheme of things, they may be expected to behave obediently. If we relax the assumption that a common purpose is involved, however, and admit the possibility (indeed, the likelihood) of conflict over goals, then coordination becomes another term for coercion. Since actors A and B disagree with goal C, they can only be "coordi-

1. For a more extended discussion of coordination see Naomi Caiden and Aaron Wildavsky, *A Constant Quantity of Tears: Planning and Budgeting in Poor Countries* (New York: John Wiley & Sons, forthcoming).

nated" by being told what to do and doing it. Coordination thus becomes a form of power.

When one bureaucrat tells another to coordinate a policy, he means that it should be cleared with other official participants who have some stake in the matter. This is a way of sharing the blame in case things go wrong (each initial on the documents being another hostage against retribution) and of increasing the predictability of securing each agreement needed for further action. Since other actors cannot be coerced, their consent must be obtained. Bargaining must take place to reconcile the differences, with the result that the policy may be modified, even to the point of compromising its original purpose. Coordination in this sense is another word for consent.

Telling another person to coordinate, therefore, does not tell him what to do. He does not know whether to coerce or bargain, to exert power or secure consent. Here we have one aspect of an apparently desirable trait of antibureaucratic administration that covers up the very problems—conflict *versus* cooperation, coercion *versus* consent —its invocation is supposed to resolve.

Everyone wants coordination—on his own terms. Invocation of coordination does not necessarily provide either a statement of or a solution to the problem, but it may be a way of avoiding both when accurate prescription would be too painful.

Coordination means getting what you do not have. It means creating unity in a city that is not unified. It means the ability to enforce agreements on employers when you are unable to do so. It means compelling federal agencies and their component parts to act in a desired manner at the right time, when achieving this purpose is precisely what you cannot do. Even when participants appear to agree with the substantive merits of a proposal, they can still oppose it or, at least, not do very much to help carry it out. One can believe that a program has merit but still think that others are more desirable. Rural areas, for example, may appear more deserving than urban ones or results there may seem more promising. One can agree with the program but believe that the wrong people are controlling the decisions or that faulty procedures have been followed. The regional organization may think that it should make critical decisions, though these might be no different from those made by its local or national affiliate. Guardians of the larger organization's integrity may believe that it will suffer if its existing procedures are violated. Full of agreement, bursting with goodwill, they may yet not take the actions required to expedite the program. Still other participants might agree on the program if they were interested in it, but they are not; for them the issue has to do with legality or compatibility with their programs and not with what the initiators think is at stake. Obtaining agreement, therefore, means first securing a meeting of the minds that the issue is what the main proponents say it is. Yet it took years for the prime movers of the EDA public works program to create mechanisms for imposing their own definition of the situation on other actors, and it is still uncertain whether they have succeeded.

Achieving coordination, again, means getting your own way. You can't learn how to do it from a slogan that tells you the way to get what you want is to already have it. Coordination has become a tautology. No one can find a solution to a problem that he is unwilling to state even to himself. No one can learn when his answers are constituted entirely by reiteration of his questions.

We began this chapter by relating the lack of organizational learning to the deficiencies of the EDA public works program in Oakland as an experiment. We then dealt with the false messiahs—bureaucracy and coordination—whose invocation only serves to obscure problems. Now it is time to bring in a real devil—the divorce of implementation from policy. Learning fails because events are caused and consequences are felt by different organizations.

Obstacles to learning have become part of the contemporary American scene in which demands for instant action interact with the federal system so as to produce separation of ideas from execution. These features render the specific events we have been discussing more familiar. Déjà vu: we have met them before. Particular facts may vary but the general story is the same: a sensational announcement from Washington on page 1, temporary local jubilation, permanent difficulties, and, perhaps years later, a small blurb on the back page signaling the end. In fact, a similar pattern of events occurs around the world when aid is dispensed by one nation to another. By bringing in an extended analogy to foreign aid, certain structural features affecting federal assistance to cities—the rival needs and circumstances of donors and recipients—stand out in bold relief.

### FOREIGN AID IN AMERICA

We can deepen our insight into the gap between the announcement of a desirable objective and its fulfillment that generates the demand for coordination by looking at the EDA's employment efforts in Oakland as analogous to problems of foreign aid. By thinking about it in this way, instead of assuming a unity of interests, we shall become aware of differences of opinion, emphasis, and timing between federal donor, host city, and the numerous organizations through which they do business. One side has limited resources to allocate; the other, limited ability to spend. They could take account of each other's limitations by designing programs geared to implementation. They might then manage to make good on their promises. Instead, both succumb to the temptation to juxtapose grand schemes for which their resources, both in terms of money and administrative capacity, are inadequate.

Failure to implement may result either from overestimation of what can be accomplished or from underestimation of ability to implement. Each error can be explained by structural features of relations between aid givers and recipients under conditions of stress.

The aid process begins in an aura of emergency: Do something! Do anything! Do it right away! Poor cities, like poor countries, are in trouble. They need so much so fast. They are always conscious that time is running out on them; hence, they are tempted to engage in short-run expedients to overcome long-run problems. Perhaps one major project, absorbing all their resources, will enable them to catch up and move ahead. Donors of aid also are caught up in the "great-leap-forward" psychology combining undue pessimism about the past with wild optimism about the future: if only they could contribute to the one big project that would turn the tide! The recipient wishes to escape the vicious cycle of poverty, the donor to be the one who helps bring this miracle about. But the ability of the donor to provide huge infusions of funds is severely limited, as is the capacity of the recipient to absorb them. Finally, they hit upon, in America, the idea of the experiment or, abroad, the demonstration project. Here is a way to join a paucity of actual resources with a maximum amount of imagination.

The view from the top is exhilarating. Divorced from problems of implementation, federal bureau heads, leaders of international agencies, and prime ministers in poor countries think great thoughts together. But they have trouble imagining the sequence of events that will bring their ideas to fruition. Other men, they believe, will tread the path once they have so brightly lit the way. Few officials down below where the action is feel able to ask whether there is more than a rhetorical connection between the word and the deed. They need money and they must get what advantage they can out of the situation. The behavior of program participants is strongly influenced by their organizational problems with giving and receiving money. The donor nation or international organization is set up to grant funds to a variety of recipients. Whether it has a lot to give or just a little, the granting organization must get rid of what it has. It is a mover of money.[2] Its task is to remove a certain amount of money from its coffers in the time period allotted. Spending, to be sure, is not the prime goal of the granting organization. It may wish to further economic growth, to see that the money is used efficiently, to reduce population. But it is difficult to determine whether these goals have been achieved, and in any event the results would not be in for a number of years. The one major criterion of success that is immediately available, accordingly, is ability to spend the allotted amount.

An important internal goal for any organization is the rationalization of its work schedule. It must secure for itself a stable flow of business so that it can allocate its time and resources. Applied to the field of foreign aid, where many of the recipient nations are disorderly and unstable, this means that the foreign donor has an interest in establishing a steady flow of projects requesting funds. Should the recipient nation be unable to supply this flow, the donor organization will stimulate it by engaging in a form of vertical integration. It sends out teams that suggest the kind of projects desired and that may even help draw them up. It seeks oases of calm and stability in the form of autonomous organizations that do not have to follow civil service regulations and that control their own funds. The donor establishes genial relationships with subunits in the recipient nation. They have a supportive relationship: one spends and the other supplies the money.

For the host country, foreign aid is both an opportunity and a problem. It is an opportunity to overcome the perennial shortage of

2. See Judith Tendler, "The Abundance of Foreign Assistance" (unpublished paper, Dept. of Economics, U.C., Irvine, 1970); and Caiden and Wildavsky, *op. cit.*

funds for investment; it is a problem because it is not easy to determine which projects should be supported and because the expenditures always include local funds that are in perpetually short supply.
To the degree that the recipient nation is not subject to powerful central direction, various autonomous organizations and ministries may
make separate arrangements with the granting organization. The
money goes to those agencies able to produce the largest number of
projects with the appropriate glossy brochures, and it is worthwhile
for them to keep a shelf of projects on hand. Where this nation is internally divided, as is often the case, it is not possible to give foreign
aid to any one segment without alienating others. Nor is it possible
to guarantee that the government in power at the time the arrangement was made will still be there when the money is spent, or that
the new government will honor the arrangements of the old.

The EDA experience in Oakland began with two features familiar
to observers of foreign aid programs—the atmosphere of crisis and
the need to spend money in a hurry. Just as it is often alleged that a
certain country will undergo revolution, flood, or famine unless
foreign aid is immediately forthcoming, so was it believed that Oakland would face race riots unless something was done. The post-
Watts atmosphere in America was heavy with foreboding. Although
no one really understood or understands today the origins of the race
riots that swept across America, speculations about the next places
likely to blow up invariably included the city of Oakland. Many
people who lived or visited there were convinced it was ripe for de-
struction. One cannot understand the actions of Foley, Bradford,
and the other people in the EDA unless one shares with them their
feeling that unless they did something immediately terrible consequences would ensue.

The supercharged emotional atmosphere favorable to immediate
action was greatly enhanced by the prevailing budgetary situation.
Funds were available in that year's budget and they would lapse unless they were committed within four months. The money had to be
moved or the opportunity to do good with it would be lost. So the
question of whether they really understood how to increase minority
employment was beside the point: they had one idea, and it was that
or nothing. The money movers did not face a choice between good
and bad actions or better and worse actions, but between some action and none. Oakland would burn, they thought, and they would

make no impact, they were certain, if they stood around and waited for better ideas. Public concern and private interest combined to force action. Their indicators of success—visible activity to reassure Oakland's black citizens and movement of money—pointed in the same direction: Action.

Faced with the necessity of moving at once, the EDA jumped at the chance of developing a relationship with the Port of Oakland. As an autonomous organization it controlled its own sources of funds and could enter into arrangements without the approval of other organizations such as the city. Besides, the port was a going concern with a competent staff and, best of all, a shelf of projects ready to go. Those already advantaged are in a position to spend money and, therefore, to receive more. By the same token, they can resist pressure to make them act in ways they deem undesirable.

Building agreement into a foreign aid situation is difficult. The donor agency must enter into working relationships with officials of the recipient polity, but it must also maintain enough distance from those officials to avoid being captured. Somehow, the distant donor must encourage diverse local institutions to work together for a common purpose. And the donor is by no means a monolithic organization; not only is the principal donor agency typically required to work with other aid-giving units, but the principal agency itself may be fragmented by differing perspectives.

The EDA was far from being the only federal organization interested in establishing connections with local bodies that would agree to spend its money. The Office of Economic Opportunity had its poverty programs (OEDCI); the Department of Housing and Urban Development (HUD) supported the local redevelopment authority; Health, Education and Welfare (HEW) dealt with the skills center; and the Department of Labor was in constant touch with the subdivisions of the State Employment Service (SES). These federal organizations all had an interest in assuring a flow of proposals they can support to whatever amount they have available. (They can also point to the flow of projects as a basis of enlarging support.) These relationships, however, were long established compared with the EDA in Oakland. It could not poach, so to speak, on the territory of these other federal organizations. Nor could it deal with the city as a whole, because the municipality was not organized to submit projects to create employment. The city was interested in saving capital expenditures[3] and was appeased rather cheaply with the Hegenberger overpass to the coliseum.

The struggle of EDA officials to comprehend the divided city of Oakland reads like a replay of the dilemmas of foreign aid officials almost any place around the world. They need official contact and approval to get their projects ratified; but they fear being labeled with the stigma of status quo, so they point first in the direction of the powers that be and then to their opponents and end up, naturally, satisfying neither one. No one knows for certain whether the city is as explosive as is claimed. No one knows who, if anyone, can really speak for the black people of the city. Amory Bradford sought out certain local militants only to be told by others that the first were not to be taken seriously. Visitors to EDA headquarters in Washington report always being asked for information on what Oakland was really like, questions that did not vary from the first visit to the last. It is not easy to grab hold of a shifting and volatile environment, particularly when the people in it do not agree on what is there, who is responsible for it, how it might be remedied, or who speaks for them.

Time and again various officials connected with the EDA bemoan the fact that there was no comprehensive economic development plan for the city. Hiring the Floyd Hunter organization was a desperate effort to produce some economic studies they could actually use. Once more we note the parallel to the insistence of donor nations (including the so-called capitalistic United States) on seeing national plans before they will spend money. Apparently there is something reassuring about seeing numbers and figures and words in a multivolumed document. Part of the insistence on an economic plan undoubtedly stems from a belief that it would do Oakland good to have it. But what the EDA people really wanted, though they were only occasionally able to verbalize it, was the political control and agreement symbolized by the plan. They were too far away and too busy with other things to dream of running the city of Oakland. They could not even imagine intervening on a constant and effective basis. No, their one devout wish was that the city would organize itself and present the EDA with a list of priorities that would include a series

3. See Frank Levy, Arnold Meltsner, and Aaron Wildavsky, "Urban Outcomes" (Oakland Project paper, 1972), chapter 3.

of well-worked-out projects that it could implement. That is why some officials spoke longingly of Mayor Daley of Chicago, who, although not exactly their favorite person, was able to impose sufficient agreement on a committee made up of minority representatives, city officials, and businessmen to produce projects that the EDA could then support, and then help the agency follow through on enforcing employment agreements. Their conclusion, expressed by a high-level EDA official, was that, "if a community can't plan for its own development and its own growth, we can't do a damn thing for them."

The complaints of federal officials about the fragmented form of government in Oakland are the equivalent of those made by foreign aid officials about the instability of regimes in developing countries. The consequences are much the same; the donor nation finds it difficult to deal with existing authorities or to know who is in authority. Just as there is more than one potential recipient within the city, however, there is also more than one potential donor whose interests may have to be reconciled. Given the institutional fragmentation of both donors and recipients, it is hard to make "agreement" or "coordination" operational.

Evidence that America has not yet lost its taste for internal foreign aid comes from Martha Derthick's study of President Johnson's "new towns" program. Like the EDA Oakland effort, the new towns program was part of an ambitious and exciting federal design. Derthick states that HUD's planners wanted

to create a community that would be a model for urban society in the second half of the twentieth century. They assumed that different social classes and races could be integrated through a shared attachment to a place and the symbols, lifestyle, and activities associated with it. With an emphasis on "participation" and "decentralization," they also sought to set new styles in social action. And they sought innovation in every aspect of planning, design, and development.[4]

The federal design was stirring, but those who drew it up did not adequately appreciate how great the difficulties of implementation would be. Federal officials were too remote from the urban scene to appreciate the mixed reception that low-income housing generates in cities or the reluctance of city councils to mix problems of race

4. Martha Derthick, *New Towns In-Town*, p. 92.

and class in view of substantial local opposition and little visible local support. The federal government's planners had thought that they could encourage local construction of public housing by offering the incentive of cheap land. But this incentive proved illusory; it was learned that there were laws on the books prohibiting disposal of land at less than fair market value. Derthick observes that "separation from local politics and administration gives policy-makers in the federal government a license to formulate ideal objectives; it may also give them a license to formulate innovative ones, for the political and administrative burdens of the innovations they conceive will be borne locally. They are free, much freer than local officials, to stand publicly for progress and high principle."[5] But after formulating high principles, federal authors have to depend on local actors for implementation; and local resistance finally made implementation of the "new towns" program impossible.

It is easy to say that federal policy makers should not overestimate the amount of support local officials can and will bring to their cause. EDA officials in Oakland felt that the employment plan would represent a commitment on the part of the port and World Airways to hire minority unemployed, but that "pressure" on the part of local officials would be forthcoming to hold these institutions to their word. (Foley and Bradford had expected that the EDA itself would enforce employment plan agreements, but subsequently the "local pressure" view became dominant at the EDA). Given the lack of power in City Hall, however, local officials had no way to exert influence on the port. Nor was the Black Caucus sufficiently organized at that time to bring the influence of potential job holders to bear. Derthick comments that when federal programs are dependent on local political actors, "whatever flaws there are in the local officials' ability to act effectively—to gather public support, to overcome opposition, to assemble an administrative organization—were liabilities for the federal government as well."[6]

In both the new towns and the Oakland EDA programs, we find similar phenomena: federal grandeur, inadequate local support, and a divorce of implementation from policy.

5. *Ibid.*, p. 94.
6. *Ibid.*, p. 88.

## TOWARD IMPLEMENTATION

We have learned one important lesson from the EDA experience in Oakland: implementation should not be divorced from policy. There is no point in having good ideas if they cannot be carried out. Stated in the form of this homily, everyone would agree. But in the EDA Oakland program, the formulation of policy was divorced from its eventual attempt at execution. From the outset the emphasis was on designing the program, obtaining initial agreement at the local level, and committing the funds. All this was done quickly, with fanfare and enthusiasm, by EDA leaders and by the agency's special Oakland task force. The later steps of implementation were felt to be "technical questions" that would resolve themselves if the initial agreements were negotiated and commitments were made. But the years have shown how those seemingly routine questions of implementation were the rocks on which the program eventually foundered.

The great problem, as we understand it, is to make the difficulties of implementation a part of the initial formulation of policy. Implementation must not be conceived as a process that takes place after, and independent of, the design of policy. Means and ends can be brought into somewhat closer correspondence only by making each partially dependent on the other.

Having observed one project that fulfilled original expectations (the health center) and two that did not (public works and business loans), we would like to suggest some ways in which policy might be designed to facilitate implementation. If policy makers were to close the gap between design and implementation by gearing programs more directly to the demands of executing them, what sorts of actions might they undertake?

First of all, an appreciation of the length and unpredictability of necessary decision sequences in implementation should lead the designers of policy to consider more direct means for accomplishing their desired ends. Since each required clearance point adds to the probability of stoppage or delay, the number of these points should be minimized wherever possible. The fact that the training program considered for Oakland required approval by nine separate organizations made it unlikely that the program would move along as quickly as its sponsors would have liked; in fact, it never did survive the hazardous round of clearances. Compared to business loans and the other public works programs, the West Oakland Health Center (see Table 10 and Figure 8) was notable for its directness. Instead of providing money to white-owned businesses who would then be required to find and hire unemployed minorities, the health center was to be run by people from the black community. By its very nature and location, this community health institution would be strongly inclined to hire minorities.

A second way of joining policy more closely to implementation would be to pay as much attention to the creation of organizational

TABLE 10: Points of Decision and Clearance Necessary for Completion of West Oakland Health Center

| Decision Points | Participants Involved | Cumulative Total of Agreements |
|---|---|---|
| 1. Submission and approval of application for funding (spring 1968) | West Oakland Health Council, Inc., EDA Oakland, EDA Washington | 3 |
| 2. Decision to allow one firm to design and construct project (June 1968) | West Oakland Health Council, Inc., US Public Health Service, EDA Washington | 6 |
| 3. Decision to approve cost overrun of $200,000 (August 1968) | EDA Washington | 7 |
| 4. Agreement on interim financing and method of paying contractors (February 1969) | West Oakland Health Council, Inc., EDA Washington | 9 |
| 5. Letting of construction contracts (February 1969) | West Oakland Health Council, Inc., Designed Facilities Corporation, EDA Washington | 12 |
| 6. Agreement on assembly of plumbing fixtures (summer 1969) | Designed Facilities Corporation, Oakland Building Department | 14 |
| Project completed: | August 20, 1969 | |

FIGURE 8. The decision path: the West Oakland Health Center

machinery for executing a program as for launching one. EDA leaders took great pains to design the best organization they could think of for approving applications, committing funds, and negotiating initial agreements. But in most of the projects they did not spend as much time ensuring that the initial commitment would be followed up by the agency; in fact, the EDA itself seemed to lose its own intense interest in the program after 1966. Although those who design programs might not generally enjoy the less exciting work of directing their implementation, a realization of the extent to which policy depends on implementation could lead such people to alter their own time perspectives and stay around for the technical details of executing a program. In the case of the health center, one of the project's most enthusiastic supporters—Public Works Director George Karras—was also in charge of much of the machinery for day-to-day implementation. Thus formulation and execution of policy were joined.

We recognize, however, that in some respects the history of the health center represents a limiting case rather than a typical one. The neighborhood supporting group managed to maintain a united front in facing the outside world. Their project was small and their purpose noble. No one wanted to oppose it; everyone—the mayor, a number of local doctors, the congressmen—wanted to support it. EDA bureaucrats dedicated themselves to making it work. Their frustrations with other programs worked to the benefit of the health center. By the time it came along, the bureaucrats were willing to eliminate obstacles that had held up earlier projects—for example, the demand for a separation of design and construction. Had the health center been much larger or subject to more visible internal conflicts, EDA bureaucrats might not have been able to use their extensive experience to provide shortcuts around, under, and through the usual obstacle course. The EDA was anxious to achieve a success in Oakland and it had enough money to construct the center. Performance, for once, equaled or exceeded promise.

Local unity, federal modesty, an excess of resources over requirements—it all sounds like too much to expect. And it is. No doubt other EDA public works programs are more typical. What advice might have been given under the actual circumstances prevailing at the time to bring policy and implementation closer together? We shall conclude by suggesting how the economic theory that lay behind the public works program could have been modified to enhance the prospects of implementation.

# 7

## Economic Theory and Program Implementation

Experience with the innumerable steps involved in program implementation suggests that simplicity in policies is much to be desired. The fewer the steps involved in carrying out the program, the fewer the opportunities for a disaster to overtake it. The more directly the policy aims at its target, the fewer the decisions involved in its ultimate realization and the greater the likelihood it will be implemented. Simplicity is, of course, not an end in itself; a fast train is worse than a slow one if it takes you in the wrong direction. Simplicity can be ignored, however, only at the peril of breakdown.

Behind the seemingly endless number of roadblocks in the path of the EDA employment program in Oakland lay deficiencies in concept. The economic theory was faulty because it aimed at the wrong target—subsidizing the capital of business enterprises rather than their wage bill. Instead of taking the direct path of paying the employers a subsidy on wages after they had hired minority personnel, the EDA program expanded their capital on the promise that they would later hire the right people. Theoretical defects exacerbated bureaucratic problems. Numerous activities had to be carried on—assessing the viability of marginal enterprises, negotiating loan agreements, devising and monitoring employment plans—that would have been unnecessary if a more direct approach had been taken.

When automobile speeds at fifty miles an hour motorcycle cop (A) starts in persuit—motorcycle hits cat (B), causing it to fall on button (C) which sets off cannon (D)— cannon ball (E) hits ivory dome of barber (F), bouncing off and knocking neck off bottle of strong acid (G)—acid drops on gold nugget (H) dissolving it—weight of kernels of corn (J) lower board (I) and fall into flower pot (K)—corn grows till it reaches height (L)— can(M) of lima beans (M)jumps at corn on account of the natural affinity for succotash—string on end of can pulls lever (O) which pushes pointer (P) into paper tank (Q) half filled with water in which sardine (R) is swimming—pointer punctures paper tank, water runs out and sardine catches severe cold from exposure—sardine contracts a very high fever that finally sets fire to paper tank and lights cigar (S).

*(Rube Goldberg cartoon, courtesy of the Bancroft Library.)*

THERE MUST BE A BETTER WAY.

SUBSIDIZING CAPITAL VERSUS LABOR

The difficulties were rooted in reliance on organizational tradition. The EDA, which had been created to deal with economically depressed regions such as Appalachia, could hardly be expected to realize that Oakland, though suffering from heavy unemployment, nevertheless lay in the midst of a prosperous region. The desire of Eugene Foley and his associates to act quickly led them to overlook ways in which cities like Oakland differ from the pattern of depressed areas. They did understand that it was insufficient merely to create economic growth; they knew they had to seek assurances that new jobs would go to the minority people in whose interest the federal money was presumably being expended. But their desire to move with the greatest possible speed persuaded them to devise a program based on promises rather than performance. Their innovation, they thought, was funneling money into a city rapidly on condition that it be used to generate the right kind of employment. Their creativity consisted in moving money and devising mechanisms of compliance after it had been spent. No one asked them whether it might have been better to give firms incentives to hire minority personnel by paying part of the cost after the men had been hired. No one asked whether Oakland fit the mold of the depressed region on which the EDA's previous public works-employment projects had been modeled.

Oakland is undergoing a transition from a manufacturing to a service center.[1] A study conducted by the city Planning Department shows that

beginning in the late 1940's and throughout the 1950's [Oakland] experienced a continued net loss of jobs in the manufacturing sector at the very same time southern Alameda County [the county in which Oakland is located] registered continued growth in these industries. . . .

But manufacturing was not the only economic activity breaking out of its traditional locational framework. The vast outlying residential development and consequent population shifts caused significant changes in the locational pattern of retail establishments. The postwar housing boom caused a major drop in the old downtown's share of retail sales. . . .

Certain elements of the "service" sector—finance, insurance, and real

1. Pp. 149–158 have been adapted from Owen McShane, "Towards a Transitional Economics: A Reappraisal of Urban Development Administration in Oakland, California," M.C.P. thesis, University of California at Berkeley, June 1970.

estate (FIRE) services, and government—never migrated to the developing outer areas as manufacturing and retailing did.[2]

Manufacturing jobs are increasingly available in Alameda County, while the nonmanufacturing jobs are available in the Oakland city core itself.

.Oakland is *not* the core city for a depressed hinterland. The East Bay is a flourishing region, and even within that larger entity Alameda County is enjoying a boom when compared to most of the nation. For Alameda County, for example, "the 15 percent rate of growth anticipated in wage and salary employment over the five years to 1971 is greater than the projected rate for the United States."[3] But this boom is not evenly distributed geographically within the county:

Between 1958 and 1966, total employment in Alameda County increased by 90,800 jobs, a growth of 28 percent over the eight year period. This rate of growth was faster than that for the five county San Francisco-Oakland Standard Metropolitan Statistical Area. However, while parts of Alameda County experienced considerable economic growth, employment in the core city, Oakland, increased by only 8,900 jobs, for a rate of 5 percent over the eight years. Only one in ten of all jobs added in the county were located in Oakland. As a consequence, the proportion of County employment located in Oakland fell from 53 percent in 1958 to 44 percent in 1966.[4]

Postwar housing expansion redistributed the population away from the dense cores, a move both accommodated and encouraged by the increase in car ownership and freeway development. Many industries followed the labor force.[5]

The result was that

In each of the four major industries that together provide 80 percent of all jobs both in the County and in Oakland (manufacturing, trade, service and government), jobs were added at a much faster rate outside Oakland than in the central city. The sharpest discrepancy in employment trends occurred in manufacturing, where Oakland lost over 9,000 jobs since 1958 (mostly to industrial areas in South County) while the County had a net gain of 13,900 manufacturing employees.[6]

2. City Planning Department, Oakland, *Options for Oakland,* p. 61.
3. California Department of Employment in cooperation with the city of Oakland 701 Project, *East Bay Manpower Survey, Alameda County, 1966–1971* (San Francisco, July 1967), p. 1.
4. *Ibid.*
5. City Planning Department, Oakland, p. 61.
6. *East Bay Manpower Survey, Alameda County,* p. 1.

Thus, the East Bay enjoys a flourishing economy, within which Alameda County is growing even more rapidly than most. The suburban areas, however, are growing more rapidly than the core and are attracting a greater share of manufacturing and retail industry as they do so. Central Oakland is increasingly having to adapt to serving the role of service center to the East Bay region.

A population that is well trained, with good access to public and private transportation, will have little difficulty in adapting to the shifts in job locations. The characteristics of a large section of Oakland's population, however, makes it peculiarly susceptible to unemployment under these circumstances. Oakland has a disproportionate share of the poor, the low skilled, and the minorities. The white suburban middle-class resident has no difficulty in learning of a job in central Oakland in its expanding service sector; he has no problem in getting into the job for interviews; and finally, he has no difficulty in commuting to the job each day, be it by car, bus, or the forthcoming rapid transit. For the poor, unskilled minority member trying to find employment after his previous manufacturing job has been relocated to the suburbs, the situation is markedly different. His informal connection with the manufacturing job market has been atrophied, for his friends and neighbors are in no better position than he. Even if he finds a job, he may not be able to commute daily, for he is either too poor to own a reliable car or the public transport system does not serve the new plant. When he turns to the expanding nonmanufacturing job market near at hand, he finds his skills are no longer in demand, his poor educational background ill fits him to learn new skills, and he faces anew the problem of overcoming racial discrimination.

The redistribution of people and jobs has left city residents at a disadvantage. According to the city Planning Department, "Almost 40 percent of all employed persons residing in Oakland were commuting to jobs outside the city. The net result of total commuter movement into and out of the city was that less than half of all Oakland jobs were filled by its residents. . . . In-commuters are disproportionately *white*. By contrast, a larger proportion of blacks than *whites* leave the city for employment. Thus, the overall relationship between commuter patterns and ethnicity indicates that Oakland is increasingly providing a home for blacks and a place of employment for *whites*."[7]

Unemployment may occur in the "depressed region" or the "distressed neighborhood." Recognition of these two types is critical to the kind of policy likely to be successful in one environment as compared with the other. Appalachia is the epitome of the depressed region. As Franklin D. Roosevelt, Jr., observed,

The problem behind Appalachia's unemployment problem is not simply that the resource potential is underdeveloped and that it lacks an industrial complex which might be diversified or amplified to make use of the unemployed. The problem is even more basic and more grave: It is that in Appalachia there exists no standard American labor force, with ready aptitudes or a diversity of basic skills; there is a deficit in the educational resources needed to raise even the level of functional literacy—let alone the level of vocational ability; and finally the region lacks the financial or physical mobility necessary for resettlement or retraining in areas of more opportunity.[8]

Appalachia is ten times the size of Switzerland, comprising 362 counties in ten states. Thousands of people live in this region and yet there is no "town"—and hence no water supply, no firehouse, no library, and no police station and hardly any beauty parlors, soda fountains, or offices where women, boys, and girls might find even part-time jobs. The weakness of the economic base of the region depresses the wealth—fiscal, social, and cultural—of all who live there. Most everyone stands to gain from any program that brings money and jobs to Appalachia. Any project that creates jobs is bound to draw on those who need them; there is no alternative, unless the project attracts skilled people to the area from outside. But the depressed region needs them, too.

In contrast to the depressed region, the distressed neighborhood exists, not separate and distant from the nation's wealth, but completely within and surrounded by it. The urban ghetto is often within two blocks of some of the highest value real estate in the nation. Industry and commerce thrive around it so that the unemployed can sit in their doors and watch the "fat cats" go to work. Typically, this distressed neighborhood lies in the heart of a growing, diversifying region that is by no means "outside the mainstream of the Nation's

7. City Planning Department, Oakland, pp. 71–72.

8. Franklin D. Roosevelt, Jr., "Appalachia: Case Study for Regional Development," in *The Manpower Revolution: Its Policy Consequences,* ed. Garth L. Mangum (New York: Doubleday, 1965), p. 397.

prosperity" but is at its very heart. Creating employment in the larger Oakland area, therefore, may bring jobs to those who can get them rather than those who need them.

According to EDA criteria, the city government jurisdiction known as Oakland qualifies as a depressed region. But former Senator Knowland disagrees,[9] and one's own common sense suggests that the East Bay region or metropolitan Oakland[10] by no means qualifies. But it is this "economic region" that must be considered when dealing with problems of unemployment and the local labor market. Under this model an appropriate observation would be that the East Bay is an area of rapid growth with a diverse economic base, a high per capita income, and so forth but in which, because of certain characteristics of the postindustrial economy and deficiencies in the labor market, many residents remain chronically unemployed, even during periods of high aggregate demand. These people are mainly found in the inner city ghettoes of Richmond and Oakland. These characteristics reduce the efficacy and leverage of many of the techniques developed by the ARA in its rural experience when they are applied to the problems of the distressed neighborhood. The problem is not one of bringing a regional economy up to the strength required to employ an underemployed population, but one of rigging a strong and well-developed metropolitan economy so as to reduce the disparity between the location and characteristics of jobs available and the location and skills of the distressed population.

As one would expect with Appalachia in mind, the Public Works and Economic Development Act outlines a program designed to develop the economy of a depressed region. The act says, "Project criteria: Projects must contribute (directly or indirectly) either to the creation of new jobs or to the alleviation of poverty. . . . Example of eligible projects: Waterworks and lines, sanitation facilities, access roads for industrial areas or potential industrial areas, public tourism facilities, and vocational schools, airports, or flood control projects for which there is a serious need but for which other federal

9. See letter from William F. Knowland to the *New York Times Magazine*, Sept. 4, 1966, p. 12.

10. For statistical evidence see "Metropolitan Oakland, Bright Spot, '66–'67" (published by the *Oakland Tribune*, n.d.).

financing is not available."[11] These examples all refer to building up infrastructure—services and capacities—to support development in a large area. The fact that this section of the act is directed toward the economies of rural areas and small towns is evident from statements by the legislators responsible for the bill. None of the presentations, submissions, hearings, and debates leading to the passing of the Public Works and Economic Development Act of 1965 ever suggests that the legislation was intended to operate in the distressed neighborhoods of flourishing regions.

When the EDA came to Oakland and funded an access road to the Oakland coliseum complex with the aim of opening up new industrial land, it was working within the intent of the act. The building of such access roads has been a major part of expenditure in depressed region programs. It was expected that hotels, motels, and restaurants providing approximately six hundred jobs would be developed along this road.[12] The emphasis on jobs per se can be explained by the tradition of evaluating infrastructure projects in depressed regions where "any job is the right job," whereas in Oakland a motel can draw its staff from the whole East Bay region. As of October 1969, the coliseum access road had created no new jobs for the hard-core unemployed.[13]

EDA policy not only favored industrial infrastructure, but also stated a clear preference for manufacturing rather than the service industry. In response to an inquiry about the possibility of the EDA lending money to hotels, Foley replied, "It is difficult to see how such enterprises create a net increase in employment and do not simply transfer employment from one part of the community to another. We're not writing off the idea. At the Small Business Administration, we funded a shopping center in South Chicago. Usually, though, we're interested in manufacturing."[14]

Again, in the industrial, or even preindustrial, economy of the depressed region, a policy favoring manufacturing makes some sense as an array of subsidiary service activities can be expected to develop around initial prime employers. But in the East Bay, such prime em-

11. U.S. Department of Commerce, E.D.A., *Facts About EDA,* Public Works and Economic Development Act, 1965. Public Law 89–136, pp. 1–2.
12. EDA internal report, p. 20.
13. McShane, p. 83.
14. From Dunsmuir meeting minutes, quoted in McShane, p. 84.

ployers already exist, and the core city locations are attractive mainly for the service sector.

If one is providing money to develop industry in a depressed region of, say, a hundred-mile diameter, one of the comforts is that for every job created directly by funding—either in the public or private sector—there will be other jobs ("spinoffs") resulting from the need to service the initial jobs. If a factory makes water pumps, extra trucks will be needed to transport the pumps, extra service stations will be needed to service the trucks, and so on. In the depressed region, all these jobs benefit the target population. There is little need to be concerned with identifying a target population and ensuring that they are the recipients of the jobs. Drawing attention to the benefits of spinoff, Senator Douglas, in a hearing before the Banking and Currency Committee in 1965, argued that a 70,000 increase in direct jobs could represent a total increase of 140,000 jobs.[15] Building a road to open up land for industrial development is sufficient. Unless potential employees are prepared to drive fifty miles from an adjoining rich region, there is little chance of the project benefiting the wrong population. Yet the problem in Oakland is precisely to assure that the jobs go to the right people.

Increased economic prosperity for a firm can lead to a significant increase in jobs if the firm is labor intensive and if the aid offered subsidizes the cost of labor—an employment subsidy. The EDA offered cheap capital. Such a program would tend to attract capital-intensive industries which, on receipt of low cost capital, would become even more capital intensive. "It seems reasonable to suppose," Clopper Almon wrote, "that a spurt in an industry's expansion, bringing with it an influx of new equipment, would quicken the rate of its [labor] productivity growth."[16] The two major recipients in the business loans program were in food processing, a highly capital-intensive industry. Both increased their employment much less than anticipated.

Any incentive to industrial growth and development, whether at the national level in the form of tax cuts or increased depreciation

15. U.S. Senate, Public Works and Economic Development Hearings before a subcommittee of the Committee on Banking and Currency, 89th Congress, 1st Session, on Titles II and IV of S 1648, May 4–7, 1965, p. 73.

16. Clopper Almon, Jr., *The American Economy to 1975* (New York: Harper and Row, 1966), p. 128.

rates or at the local level in the form of low cost loans or capital grants, is likely to reduce the labor intensiveness of industry unless countervailing pressures are brought to bear. In explaining the hostility of other bakers to the EDA loan to Colombo Bakery, Mr. Mueller said, "After all, as far as they were concerned, EDA was providing cheap money for Colombo to fully automate its plant . . . !"[17]

Offering low cost capital to attract firms to depressed regions makes more sense in that labor costs tend to be low in such areas anyway; the firm is offered both cheap capital and cheap labor. This combination is unlikely to exist in the union-controlled metropolitan areas. The capital subsidy program makes sense in the depressed region where there is a surplus of semiskilled labor left behind by the departure of another industry and where it is a shortage of capital that prevents firms setting up in the area. In the flourishing regions such as the East Bay, finance is ordinarily no real problem to the large employers, and the intention is not so much to encourage industry to choose an abnormal location as to induce it to draw on a different sector of the population for its labor force. Let us take a brief look at an approach to the problem in Great Britain that focuses on subsidizing wages.

In 1967 the Department of Economic Affairs in Great Britain introduced a proposal for a regional employment premium. The essence of the proposal was "that the existing grants and other assistance for capital investment should be supplemented for a period of years by payments towards the labour cost of manufacturing industry in the Development Areas."[18] The department directly addressed the need to subsidize labor if capital subsidy is not to further aggravate the structural unemployment caused by increases in labor productivity:

The proposed assistance towards labour costs would act in conjunction with the existing incentives to capital investment. It would help to meet the criticism which is sometimes levelled against special regional investment incentives that, in the absence of assistance towards labour costs, they tend to tip the balance in favour of locating capital-intensive projects in areas of labour

17. McShane interview with Ken Mueller of the OEDF, April 16, 1970.
18. Great Britain, Department of Economic Affairs, H.M. Treasury, *The Development Areas: A Proposal for a Regional Employment Premium* (London, 1967), para. 18.

surplus rather than in areas of labour shortage. The investment grants by themselves could not be further raised to produce an additional stimulus comparable with the effect of the proposed employment premium—if only because the total of capital expenditure capable of attracting grant is much smaller than the labour costs which would attract employment premium. In manufacturing industry the annual wage and salary bill is about five times the total annual investment and about seven times the annual investment in machinery.[19]

The employment premium is "across the board"—that is, any manufacturing employer in a development area receives the subsidy on all wages paid. Opinion in the United States would probably reject such a "loose" program that gives payments irrespective of the target population. An employment premium in the United States, therefore, would have to be paid only to those employers who have employed statistically defined hard-core unemployed.

John Kain outlined such a tight wage subsidy program in his presentation to the congressional Joint Economic Committee. The essentials of his scheme were that the employment service would simply certify workers who have been unemployed beyond a certain period of time (the long-term unemployed) for participation in the program. Any employer hiring one of these certified workers would receive an hourly cash subsidy. "There should be an increasing scale depending on the worker's duration of unemployment, so that firms would have a stronger incentive (larger cash subsidy) for hiring the really hard-core unemployed. . . . There should be a declining subsidy for weeks worked on the presumption that the productivity of workers increases with training and experience on the job."[20] Experimenting with these rates over a period of time should allow the most effective scales to be established.

In accord with his conviction that programs should be designed to reduce the social and economic isolation of the ghetto, Kain "would prefer a wage subsidy that would apply only to the hiring of the long-term unemployed by suburban employers—more specifically those

19. *Ibid.*, para. 28.
20. U.S. Congress, *Employment and Manpower Problems in the Cities: Implications of the Report of the National Advisory Commission on Civil Disorders,* Hearings before the Joint Economic Committee, Congress of the United States, 90th Congress, 2nd Session, May-June 1968, Statement by John F. Kain, Dept. of Economics, Harvard University and the MIT-Harvard Joint Center for Urban Studies, p. 66.

located further than a certain minimum distance from the ghetto."
However, he admits "to the logic, on narrow cost effectiveness
grounds, of a flexible wage subsidy available to firms . . . anywhere
in the metropolis."[21]

In his journal and in interviews, Amory Bradford expressed the
wish to see large corporations such as General Motors take an interest in the EDA. One reason that such corporations show little interest
is that the agency offers the wrong incentives. The Survey of Current
Business observed that "three-fifths of all capital funds used by cor-
porate business in the postwar period has been derived from internal
sources, i.e., retained earnings and depreciation allowances. An additional one-fifth has been raised in long-term markets, . . . while the
remainder has involved increases in short-term debt, principally accounts payable and bank debt."[22] It would be difficult to argue that,
given these conditions, a large corporation would be unable to find
financing through regular channels, and this presumably explains
why Bradford was unable to interest large employers. A subsidy on
wages, however, may well be an incentive to them precisely because
they do employ so many men and in jobs that typically require short
training periods.

One of the most attractive aspects of any labor subsidy or employment premium is that it is paid out only on performance. Capital subsidy plans are, however, always paid out on a promise. The applicant
says, "If you give me a low cost loan of $100,000, then I shall employ
twenty hard-core unemployed." What happens is all too likely to follow the pattern described by a black woman to whom Bradford talked
about the employment plan machinery:

Let me get this straight. You have some employer, who files a Plan saying
he will employ twenty of our people. We approve his plan, and he starts up
with your money. But then he chisels a little bit, and only employs eighteen,
and takes two others from outside, maybe his cousins or something. Does
this committee then say, "You fire those two, and take on two of ours"?
And if he won't, then you call his loan, and put him out of business, and the
other eighteen lose their jobs? I don't like the sound of that.[23]

21. *Ibid.*
22. U.S. Department of Commerce, *Survey of Current Business,* September 1957, p. 8.
23. Bradford, p. 165.

The employer was, in fact, more likely to employ only five rather than twenty new men because he substituted new capital for labor. He could claim good faith but add that "things hadn't quite worked out as expected." Bearing in mind Almon's anticipated increase in labor productivity with any rapid increase in investment, it would prove difficult to demonstrate bad faith. The dilemma of performance *versus* promise was to plague the EDA throughout its operation in Oakland. A labor subsidy, which pays on performance, avoids these problems altogether and has the attractive characteristic that failure of the program costs no money.

"Payment on performance" is a useful premise on which to base employment policy in distressed areas. One of the advantages of an employment subsidy is that money is paid out only on performance, that is, the hiring of a worker and if no workers are hired, then no money is spent—an appealing attribute for the taxpayer. If policy analysts carry bumper stickers, they should read, "Be Simple! Be Direct!" or "PAYMENT ON PERFORMANCE."

Our preferred economic theory has been proposed with the invaluable benefit of hindsight. Had we been around at the time, we might not have thought of it. Had we been subjected to the same extreme time pressure as the actual participants in the public works and business loans programs, all thought of alternatives might have been driven from our minds. The fact that the legislation establishing the EDA lacked specific reference to (though it did not prohibit) wage subsidies might have contributed to the lack of innovation. It may also be that a program to subsidize labor precisely because it was innovative might have run up against as many or even more obstacles than the other programs. Indeed, it might not have been able to get off the ground at all.

We would like to believe that legislators and administrators fully cognizant of the difficulties of implementation would have cast about for simpler and more direct methods of accomplishing the desired result. Under the self-imposed necessity of undertaking immediate action, they might not have considered the differences between a depressed neighborhood and a depressed region. But they would have searched first and foremost for a program that would connect their activities with the production of jobs, avoiding intermediary steps like the plague. This is a suggestion for the future. Our purpose, in any event, is not to lay blame for perfectly understandable error but to suggest how policy might have been improved by making implementation a part of its essential conception.

## A WORD OF CAUTION

On the side of substantive policy recommendations, we may have overestimated the likely effectiveness of a labor subsidy. It would not be difficult to find plausible arguments against our suggestions. Consider, for instance, applying the literature on the so-called dual labor market to the problem at hand.[24] The central idea is that poor people with little skill (often black males) are confined to a set of jobs characterized by low wages and status and lack of opportunity. There is no normal path of advancement for these workers within the firm's employment structure. Their turnover is high. This turnover is part of a mutually reinforcing process. Employers count on an unstable work force for the jobs, so they are designed in such a way that there are frequent hirings through "shape-ups," where the men must appear in person on the spot. Not much time is lost, therefore, when one man quits and another man is hired. Under these circumstances, a firm is not likely to invest much in training or anything else affecting the employee. At the same time, the bad qualities of the jobs and the ease with which men go from one to another—nothing is lost in the transition since the jobs have no seniority attached —means that the workers themselves develop capricious behavior, quitting frequently, working irregularly, and thereby completing the self-fulfilling prophecy of both employer and employee. The latter expects to be laid off and treated badly, so he leaves; and the former, expecting his workers to be unreliable, gives them scant consideration and is not surprised to discover that they live up to his predictions.

How would a policy of subsidizing wages fit into such a differential market? To subsidize everyone would be inefficient because there would undoubtedly be money spent on people whom the firm would have hired anyway. A more selective plan might still run into similar difficulties. A firm might merely substitute "certified hard-core unemployed" for people of equal skills whom they otherwise would

24. See, in this connection, Michael Piore and Peter Doeringer, *Internal Labor Markets and Manpower Analysis* (Lexington, Mass.: D.C. Heath, 1971).

have hired. Making certain that the increment of employment generated by the subsidy is real and goes to the people intended is no simple matter. Moreover, since turnover is a big problem in the market, the idea of diminishing the subsidy over time might prove counterproductive. It might make more sense to give a larger subsidy the longer a man stays on the job, thus rewarding the firm for reducing turnover. Naturally, this approach would prove expensive. Without carrying the discussion further, enough has been said to suggest that there is no easy road to creating long-term jobs for the hard-core unemployed.

On the political side, the American federal system will continue to pose severe problems for policies initiated by the national government. After studying the pitfalls encountered in implementing Title I (compensatory education) of the Elementary and Secondary Education Act, Jerome T. Murphy arrives at judgments similar to our own:

To blame the problems on timidity, incompetence, or "selling out" is to beg the question. I have identified a number of contributing causes: the reformers were not the implementers; inadequate staff; a disinclination to monitor; a law and tradition favoring local control; and absence of pressure from the poor. The primary cause, however, is political. The federal system—with its dispersion of power and control—not only permits but encourages the evasion and dilution of federal reform, making it nearly impossible for the federal administrator to impose program priorities; those not diluted by Congressional intervention can be ignored during state and local implementation.[25]

No one supposes that the federal system is going to disappear. If the federal principle maintains its vitality, then it means precisely that state and local organizations must be able to oppose, delay, and reject federal initiatives. When these kinds of actions can no longer be undertaken, there is no state or local independence and hence no operative federalism. The form might still be visible but the substance will have disappeared. American cities may become more internally cohesive, but they probably will not. They may all be alike, so that knowledge of one can be extended to the others, but it would be hard to find anyone who would bet on it. Consequently, formula-

25. Jerome T. Murphy, "Title I of ESEA: The Politics of Implementing Federal Education Reform," *Harvard Educational Review* 41 (1971): 60.

tors of federal programs will be faced with cities of uncertain unity and will find it difficult to gather accurate and up-to-date political intelligence about them. No matter how the federal government is organized and reorganized, virtually all social programs will cut across the jurisdictions of different bureaus, departments, and overhead agencies. While the number of clearances could be cut down by organizing with a single set of programs in mind, there is no organizational arrangement that will minimize clearances for all programs, past and future. New entrants are likely to find, as did the EDA in Oakland, that they must fit into arrangements that have been made with other purposes in mind. The requirement that the Economic Development Administration and the Small Business Administration collaborate in the administration of loans programs, for instance, added new clearance points and an inherently antagonistic relationship to an already difficult program. Getting one agency to assist another in this way met the value of reducing overlap and duplication of personnel, but it was not helpful for immediate programmatic purposes.

Moreover, the EDA itself could not have acted unilaterally to reduce the number of clearance points. Other federal actors, whose consent was uncertain and whose attention to the problem at hand was minimal—Congress and the Budget Bureau—were required to act before certain previously necessary steps could be omitted. Finally, there may be people who think that someone can issue a ukase forbidding undue haste in the design of federal programs, but we think that the tendency will be extremely difficult to resist. We still believe that difficulties of implementation can be mitigated, but we urge continued skepticism when anyone suggests that inherent features of political life can be summarily abolished.

# Appendix 1

## EDA CHRONOLOGY

### 1965

*August 26* Passage of the Public Works and Economic Development Act.

*October* Eugene Foley appointed assistant secretary of commerce in charge of the EDA.

*December* Short visit to Oakland by Foley and Amory Bradford; they meet with black community groups but do not see the mayor.

### 1966

*January 28–29* Dunsmuir House conference between EDA officials and Oakland business and government leaders. Foley commits at least $15 million.

*February* Bradford conducts extensive interviews with business, labor, and political leaders to form an acceptable employment policy.

*March* Foley approves employment plan idea.

*April 29* Announcement by Foley of $23 million in public works projects.

*October 5* Foley resigns.

*November 12* Employment Plan Review Board Committee approves World Airways plan; Bradford leaves.

## 1967

*January* Charles Patterson takes over as EDA Oakland representative.

*January 27* Port of Oakland decides to move terminal project to new location, thus ending a controversy about filling material at the previous location.

*May 6* Port signs agreement with Charles Luckman and Associates to design airline hangar.

## 1968

*April 1* Navy complains about flight safety hazards at marine terminal.

*April 2* Charles Luckman and Associates notify the port of a substantial cost overrun on the airline hangar; the port requests additional funding from the EDA.

*April 7* Port submits to the EDA a plan for a revolving restaurant at the marine terminal.

*June* EDA agrees to fund the construction of the West Oakland Health Center.

*June* World Airways Compliance Report shows drop in total number of minority employed from 12y to 111.

*August* U.S. General Accounting Office is critical of the EDA's grant and loan arrangements with the Port of Oakland.

*December 23* Charles Patterson is replaced as EDA Oakland representative by Hugh Taylor; Patterson becomes vice-president of World Airways.

## 1969

*Early February* Parties meet to sign a contract for construction of the West Oakland Health Center.

*February 26* EDA head Ross Davis denies the request for additional funding for hangar project.

*April 4* Robert A. Podesta replaces Davis as assistant secretary of commerce for EDA.

*April 7* The navy and the port finally resolve their differences on construction of the terminal.

*December* Contracts are awarded for construction of the terminal.

*December 11* EDA turns down the port's request for funds for the proposed revolving restaurant at the marine terminal.

### 1970

*February 12* EDA notifies the port that final plans and specifications for a hangar costing *less* than $9.5 million will have to be submitted by December 31, 1970, and that employment guarantees will also have to be made.

*April 8* The port hires a new architect for the hangar project.

*May 15* World Airways submits an affirmative action plan, but it is criticized by federal employment offices.

*June 30* EDA approves preliminary plans and specifications for the hangar which set the cost at $9.2 million.

### 1971

*May* Terminal completed.

*June* Contracts for constructing hangar are let.

# Appendix 2.

## USE OF "IMPLEMENTATION"
## IN SOCIAL SCIENCE LITERATURE

There is (or there must be) a large literature about implementation in the social sciences—or so we have been told by numerous people. None of them can come up with specific citations to this literature, but they are certain it must exist. Surely, they will say, the vast scholarly attention paid to poverty programs and efforts to secure compliance in the field of civil rights has generated work on problems of implementation. It must be there; it should be there; but in fact it is not. There is a kind of semantic illusion at work here because virtually everything ever done in public policy or public administration must, in the nature of things, have some bearing on implementation. Analytical study (as opposed to mere mention) of implementation seems so eminently reasonable that few can imagine it does not exist. Everyone is aware, certainly, of the widespread concern about the inability to implement governmental programs. Nevertheless, except for the few pieces mentioned in the body of this book, we have been unable to find any significant analytic work dealing with implementation.

How shall we persuade others that it is fruitless to look for a literature that does not exist, or that we cannot connect our work with nonexistent analyses by others? It is a little like searching for the little man who isn't there. It is always more difficult to establish a negative rather than a positive relationship. While we cannot hope to provide conclusive evidence (after all, there can always be something we have overlooked) we do hope to be persuasive beyond the mere assertion that there is no analytic literature on implementation.

Where might literature on implementation be found if it did exist? We cannot be expected to search everywhere, so we must pick reasonable targets of opportunity. We can scan the periodical indexes for mention of implementation or a reasonable synonym, such as execution. We may also surmise that if a literature did exist it should be cited in textbooks on public administration. Finally, we can choose two broad areas of policy—poverty programs and civil rights—to see if any of the material we can locate pays attention to implementation.

Now there are various gradations of the appearance and nonappearance of implementation. Should neither the word "implementation" nor any reasonable synonym appear in the work in question, we may safely conclude that the subject has not been treated. Should the word appear but not be defined, we might agree that the author is interested in it but that it is not very important in his context. If the concept of implementation appears and is carefully defined, but is not used analytically to make empirical statements about the word or otherwise to illuminate the subject, then it may be important to the author but it is not used in an analytic way that can be put together with other work on the subject. Actually, despite these fine distinctions, the vast bulk of the material at which we have looked fails the simplest tests. Either it does not use "implementation" at all, or the concept is undefined, or the word is mentioned in passing. No work we have consulted, except for those cited in the manuscript, makes analytic use of implementation.

## PERIODICAL INDEXES

Research on implementation is primarily conspicuous by its absence. Extensive investigations in the University of California Main Library at Berkeley, the Boalt Law Library, the Institute of Governmental Studies Library, the Kelsen Graduate Social Science Library, the Education-Psychology Library and the Institute for Research on Poverty Library at the University of Wisconsin, as well as consultation with faculty members, indicated a sparse research crop.[1] A large number of abstracts and reference works were consulted with little success:

*International Political Science Abstracts,* 1966–1971, no articles cited under implementation or execution, either in the general index or under "United States."

*Political Science Series,* nothing in the main volumes or the 1968–1970 supplements.

*Sociological Abstracts, Humanities and Social Science Abstracts, International Bibliography of Social Sciences,* all list nothing either under general or political science headings for implementation.

*American Doctoral Dissertations,* under Political Science, Public Administration, reveals nothing of interest except the Mosher dissertation on which part of *ESEA: The Office of Education Administers a Law* is based.

*Psychological Abstracts,* under Personnel and Industrial Psychology, Management and Organization, has a regular listing of organization theory articles, none of which mention implementation or seem directly related to implementation.

### POVERTY

*Poverty in the United States During the 1960's: A Bibliography,* by Dorothy Campbell Tompkins (Institute of Governmental Studies, 1970) has a total of 8,338 citations, and was lacking in any material directly relating to implementation. Although poverty studies is an area extensively codified with thousands of citations and a number of excellent bibliographies, the vast majority of these articles and books deal with the problem of poverty per se, with much discussion of specific policies such as the negative income tax. No scholarly studies cover implementation. The few items by practitioners and consultants view implementation as program initiation rather than program execution. Two California papers dealing with implementation highlights this emphasis. The first, "Implementation of the Economic Opportunity Act of 1964: The Role of the State," was published by the California State Office of Economic Opportunity

1. Failing to discover relevant literature, Wildavsky asked two graduate students (Karen Scott in Political Science and Jon Twichell in the Graduate School of Public Policy) to continue the search. Scott covered the texts on public administration and Twichell did the periodical indexes and the fields of poverty and civil rights.

in 1965 and is essentially a justification for the state OEO office. Another article (which appeared in the February 1972 issue of the *California Journal*) is titled "Legislative Hearings Spotlight Failure to Implement New State-Federal Child Care Programs" and is concerned with failure to get started because of the interbureau rivalry between the California Education and Social Welfare departments over funding of federal child care.

Another item is typical of the noninvestigation of program implementation. A Griffenhagen-Kroeger, Inc. report to the OEO on state technical assistance (STA) is a straightforward look at these STA units. The report recommends state coordination of OEO activities, more program development, technical assistance, monitoring, and research. Although there are passing comments about interagency rivalries, other problems of program implementation are not discussed.

## CIVIL RIGHTS

There has been an extensive and expanding inquiry into the compliance and enforcement aspects of civil rights legislation, an area akin to implementation. The operating definition of compliance with these laws seems to be that one can leap from policy intent to program success via strong staff, assertive leadership, and stringently enforced rules. Successful implementation is assumed to naturally follow from these. Inadequate enforcement or lax individuals are the only reasons for unsuccessful implementation; compliance is what "ought to be."

For instance, *Title VI, One Year After: A Study of Health and Welfare Services in the South,* published by the United States Commission on Civil Rights in 1966, specifically found that written agreements had been secured but segregation continued, and that HEW failed to push for compliance, failed to adopt adequate review and compliance procedures, and failed to provide states and localities with help. Their specific recommendations were: immediately apply sanctions, use surveys and field inspectors to pinpoint discrimination, establish affirmative goals, and set up regular reporting and program evaluation systems.

A later series of studies goes on in the same vein. "Contract Compliance and Equal Employment Opportunity in the Construction

Industry," the transcript of the Massachusetts State Civil Rights Commission hearings in 1969, pointed out the lack of compliance officers for the hundreds of millions of dollars of federal construction contracts in New England. In questioning the head of the New York City program, compliance problems were characterized as "Commitment—the lack of it." A civil rights report to George Schultz, Secretary of Labor (in 1969) on contract compliance cited operational difficulties in the areas of staffing and enforcement procedures. This was basically another recitation of inadequacies rather than a discussion of the many facets of implementation.

This series of reports culminated in *Federal Civil Rights Enforcement,* a massive document from the Civil Rights Commission in 1970, which surveyed the status of civil rights compliance in all areas of federal influence, including many government agencies. This report, good enough for page 1 in the *New York Times* when it was released, was taken to task by Nathan Glazer in *The Public Interest* (no. 23, spring 1971). Titled "A Breakdown in Civil Rights Enforcement?" Glazer's article contrasts the conclusions of the commission report with the immensity of the problem, the increased federal compliance staff, and the difficulties of implementing the civil rights charge. Glazer touches on a number of the broad implementation problems that affect this issue.

The Civil Rights Commission has issued a one-year follow-up that assesses performance and cautions against confusing announced intentions with implementation. Again, the operating assumption appears to be that there are no problems with compliance that stronger enforcement cannot solve.

## OPERATIONS RESEARCH

Operations Research (OR) has traditionally defined implementation as the selling of an OR scheme to a client, rather than the actual putting into practice of that scheme. Armed with that rather specific definition, Jon H. B. M. Huysmans asserts in his thesis on *The Implementation of Operations Research* that bibliographies and subject indexes in the field (such as James H. Batchelor, *OR: An Annotated Bibliography)* carry surprisingly few references to implementation. His was the only book (*The Implementation of Operations Research,* publications in operations research, no. 19; New

York: Wiley-Interscience, 1970) to use the term "implementation" in both the table of contents and the index. The author writes that "an operations research recommendation is implemented if the manager or managers affected by the recommendation adopt the research results in essence and continue to use them as long as the conditions underlying the research apply" (p. 1).

Paul Stillson ("Implementation of Problems in Operations Research," *Operations Research,* Vol. 11-1, Jan.-Feb. 1963) discusses OR implementation on two levels, (1) when it is "sold" to management and (2) when it is effectively put into operation. The article describes an operations research problem that was successfully implemented in the first case (it was sold to management), but which the company later found impossible to put into operation.

PUBLIC ADMINISTRATION

Use of the term in public administration texts generally falls into a pattern. It is usually found in the introduction which defines the scope of public administration, with implementation presented as the end product of administrative efforts or as co-extensive with public administration itself. It is also found in discussions on policy planning and legislation with implementation being the end to be kept in mind as policy or legislation is being constructed. Implementation is never formally defined or taken as a major concept or process to be studied or explained. Needless to say, the term is never followed by citations to literature on the subject.

E. N. Gladden (*The Essentials of Public Administration*; London: Staples Press, 1958), in discussing essential aspects of public administration, refers to "the stages of decision, of preparation and of execution" (p. 20). In this context, implementation is synonymous with execution. The public administration texts surveyed are basically concerned with the first two stages rather than the implementation of policy. Let us consider the major texts one at a time.

Catheryn Secker-Hudson, *Organization and Management: Theory and Practice* (Washington, D.C.: American University Press, 1955). In the chapter entitled "Policy Formation and Re-formation" administrative implementation is briefly discussed in terms of turning a law into a program: "He [the administrator] writes in the gaps; makes the rules to bridge in interstices in the law; and promulgates regulations, some of which are more important to the citizens than the law itself" (p. 69). The term "implementation" is used quite frequently in this text. Three examples of its use include a description of the control of administrative agencies over laws: "The vital factor of timing implementation of the law—even the rate of speed in implementation, may have the effect of changing the outcome or even defeating the intention of the law" (p. 69). And there are two subheads within the chapter: "Is the plan economical in terms of resources needed to implement it?" (p. 108). "Plans, when ready for implementation, should be divisible into sub-parts that can be reassembled" (p. 111). The term is never defined, however, nor is the substance behind it subjected to analysis.

Herbert A. Simon, *Administrative Behavior* (New York: Mac-Millan, 1945). Simon uses "implementation" in the introduction of his book to define other terms.

In so far as decisions lead toward the selection of final goals, they will be called "value judgments"; so far as they involve the implementation of such goals they will be called "factual judgments" [p. 5].

The concept of *purposiveness* involves a notion of a hierarchy of decisions —each step downward in the hierarchy consisting in an implementation of the goals set forth in the step immediately above [p. 5].

James C. Charlesworth, *Governmental Administration* (New York: Harper, 1951). Implementation appears in the table of contents of this book as the title of chapter 5, "Implementation of Judicial Controls over Administration." The discussion that follows, however, does not mention the term again. Otherwise, the term is mentioned elsewhere only in passing: "To implement the Act, the Civil Service Commission appointed a distinguished Board of Examiners to assist in filling 200 additional hearing examiner positions" (p. 163). "The circular letter . . . is used when the central chief wishes to explain or implement a more formal regulation" (p. 287).

Ira Sharkansky, *Public Administration* (Chicago: Markham, 1970). Sharkansky uses the word but goes no further:

. . . it is the administrator who generally implements the precise statute that is enacted by the legislature or who makes the actual delivery of public service [p. 8].

This feature [client-participation] has recently attracted considerable public attention as it has been implemented through community action programs of the U.S. Office of Economic Opportunity [p. 76].

[In describing the opportunities that interest groups seize on to express themselves on agency policy] 2. Where the administrators can delay the implementation of their policy without causing substantial harm [p. 183].

E. N. Gladden, *The Essentials of Public Administration* (London: Staples Press, 1958). Several writers appear to think of implementation as synonymous with (or even broader than) public administration itself. If implementation is everything in general, then it apparently need be nothing in particular, and is not discussed further. In the conclusion of his book, Gladden discussed "A Philosophy of Public Administration?" the third section of which involved implementation: "3) Public Administration is concerned not with policy-making but with technical processes needed for the effective implementation of policy." In other places Gladden writes, without further discussion, that

. . . Responsibility for the implementation of a particular sector of the executive policy is usually at this level assigned by the executive to one of its own members [p. 68].

Thus in a welfare state . . . the administrative implementation of . . . policy may be restricted by the inability of the administration to obtain the services of sufficient persons with sufficiently high administrative capacities [p. 71].

John Pfiffner and Robert Prethus, *Public Administration,* 4th edition (New York: Roland Press, 1960). The authors use implementation to define the nature of public administration. "Public administration involves the implementation of public policy which has been outlined by representative political bodies" (p. 4). "Public administration can also be viewed as a social process, charged with implementing great ends" (p. 6).

Elsewhere, in a subhead in chapter 3 entitled "Implementing Social Change" (p. 47), the authors view implementation as part of bureaucratic power or discretion:

The better the bureaucracy becomes at developing systematic techniques of forming and implementing policy, the greater its power for resisting the claims of special interests [p. 48].

Bureaucratic influence over policy implementation is also significant, ranging from virtual nullification of some legislation to the limited discretion involved in administering a detailed statute [p. 55].

Herbert Simon, Donald Smithburg, and Victor Thompson, *Public Administration* (New York: Knopf, 1950). The subtitle in chapter 21, "Strategy and Planning," called "Implementing Planning Goals" includes a discussion of implementation in the context of resistance to change. This short and general account is the most extensive we have been able to find:

The successful planner must understand the types of changes in behavior that are resisted so that he can avoid them or plan ways for overcoming the resistances. . . . Here we will only identify the principal types and describe them briefly: 1) inertia; 2) community or personal mores and beliefs; 3) personal self-interest; 4) the desire to be rational; and 5) the dislike of subordination [p. 440].

Fritz Morstein Marx, ed., *Elements of Public Administration* 2d ed. (Englewood Cliffs, N.J.: Prentice-Hall, 1959). Under the subhead "Statutory Implementation" (p. 163), is a discussion of the role of the Bureau of the Budget. Morstein Marx makes no further mention of implementation.

Leonard D. White, *Public Administration,* 4th ed. (New York: MacMillan, 1955). A historical and descriptive survey of public administration, includes case studies which discuss the scope of public administration and the growth of individual agencies. There is no mention of implementation.

Harold Stein, ed., *Public Administration and Policy Development* (New York: Harcourt, Brace, 1952). A book of case studies, concerned basically with the formation of policy on both the political and administrative levels. The postscript to each case records the success or failure of the implementation of the plan but does not use the term itself.

The following books did not mention implementation:

R. Joseph Novograd, Gladys O. Dimock, and E. Marshall Dimock, *Casebook in Public Administration* (New York: Holt, Rinehart, and Winston, 1969).

John D. Millett, *Management in the Public Service: The Quest for Effective Performance* (New York: McGraw-Hill, 1954).

Charles O. Jones, *An Introduction to the Study of Public Policy* (Belmont, California: Wadsworth, 1970).

Marshall and Gladys Dimock, *Public Administration* (New York: Rinehart, 1953).

Dwight Waldo, *Ideas and Issues in Public Administration* (New York: McGraw-Hill, 1955).

# Bibliography

Almon, Clopper, Jr. *The American Economy to 1975: An Interindustry Forecast.* New York: Harper & Row, 1966.

Bradford, Amory. *Oakland's Not for Burning.* New York: McKay, 1968.

Caiden, Naomi and Aaron Wildavsky. *A Constant Quantity of Tears: Planning and Budgeting in Poor Countries.* (New York: John Wiley & Sons, forthcoming.)

California Department of Employment, Coastal Area, Research and Statistics Section, in cooperation with City of Oakland 701 Project. *East Bay Manpower Survey, Alameda County, 1966–1971.* San Francisco, July 1967.

City of Oakland. Charter. Oakland, 1969.

———. *Financial Capability Study, Part One, 1968–69.*

———. City Planning Department. *Options for Oakland: A Summary Report on the Oakland 701 Project.* OCPD 198, December 1969.

Derthick, Martha, *New Towns In-Town.* Washington, D.C.: Urban Institute, 1972.

Great Britain. Department of Economic Affairs. H. M. Treasury. *The Development Areas: A Proposal for a Regional Employment Premium.* London: Her Majesty's Stationery Office, 1967.

Levitan, Sar. *Federal Aid to Depressed Areas: An Evaluation of the Area Redevelopment Administration.* Baltimore: Johns Hopkins University Press, 1964.

Levy, Frank, Arnold Meltsner, and Aaron Wildavsky. "Urban Outcomes: Education, Libraries, and Streets." Unpublished U.C. Oakland Project Paper, 1972.

Mangum, Garth L., ed., *The Manpower Revolution: Its Policy Consequences.* Garden City, N.Y.: Doubleday, 1965.

McShane, Owen. "Towards a Transitional Economics: A Reappraisal of Urban Development Administration in Oakland, California." Master of city planning thesis, University of California at Berkeley, June 1970.

Montgomery, Douglas G. "The Federal Delivery System: Impact on the Community. A Case Study of EDA and the West Oakland Health Center." Paper delivered at the American Political Science Association annual meeting, Los Angeles, 1970.

*Oakland Tribune.* "Metropolitan Oakland, Bright Spot '66–'67." no date.

Resnikoff, Louise. "EDA in Oakland: An Evaluation." Unpublished U.C. Oakland Project paper, October 1969.

Roosevelt, Franklin D., Jr. "Appalachia: Case Study for Regional Development." In *The Manpower Revolution: Its Policy Consequences,* ed. Garth L. Mangum. Garden City, N.Y.: Doubleday, 1965.

Stanford Research Institute. *Human Resources Development for Oakland: Problems and Policies.* Menlo Park, 1968.

Sundquist, James L. *Politics and Policy: The Eisenhower, Kennedy, and Johnson Years.* Washington, D.C.: Brookings Institution, 1968.

Tendler, Judith. "The Abundance of Foreign Assistance." Unpublished paper, Department of Economics, U.C., Irvine, 1970.

U.S. Department of Commerce. Economic Development Administration. Urban Affairs Division, Office of Policy Coordination. *EDA in Oakland, California: An Analysis.* October 1968. (Referred to in footnotes as EDA internal report.)

U.S. Department of Commerce, Office of Business Economics. *Survey of Current Business,* vol. 37, no. 9 (September 1957).

U.S. Congress. House. Committee on Public Works. Public Works and Economic Development Act, 1965. H.R. 6991, 89th Congress, 1st session.

———. ———. ———. Economic Development Administration's Reply to Subcommittee's First Interim Report and Related Matters. Special Subcommittee on Economic Development Programs. Hearing. 90th Congress, 1st Session, April 11, 1967.

———. Joint Economic Committee Hearings. 90th Congress, May 28, 29; June 4, 5, 6, 1968. *Employment and Manpower Problems in the Cities: Implications of the Report of the National Advisory Commission on Civil Disorders.* 2nd Session.

U.S. Congress. Senate. *Congressional Record,* May 26, 1965. "Public Works and Development Act of 1965," pp. 11777–11799.

———. ———. Public Works Committee. Public Works and Economic Development Act, 1965. Hearings. 89th Congress, 1st Session, S1648 (10702) April 26-May 3, 1965. May 26, 1965.

———. ———. Banking and Currency Committee. Public Works and Economic Development Subcommittee Hearings. 89th Congress, 1st Session, on S1648 (10671). May 4, 5, 6, and 7, 1965.

U.S. Public Law 89-136, Public Works and Economic Development Act of 1965, 89th Congress, 1st Session.

University of California Survey Research Center. *Poverty and Poverty Programs in Oakland: Selected Results from the 701 Household Survey of Oakland.* William L. Nicholls II, Study Director. Berkeley: Survey Research Center, 1967.

# Index